FATHER'S

INFLUENCE

ON

CHILDREN

Father's Influence on Children

Marshall L. Hamilton

Nelson-Hall ▥ Chicago

Library of Congress Cataloging in Publication Data

Hamilton, Marshall L
  Father's influence on children.

  Bibliography: p.
  Includes index.
  1. Fathers. 2. Father and child. I. Title.
HQ756.H35   301.42'7   76-41799
ISBN 0-88229-142-4

Manufactured in the United States of America.

To my father who died too young, and
to Sally and our children.

contents

preface

In recent years behavioral scientists have noted great discrepancy between commonly held views and the actual findings of careful research, concerning the influence of fathers upon their children. The articles dealing with this problem are scattered through various scholarly journals, with the result that only a relative handful of people are aware of how underestimated the father's influence is. The intent of this book is to gather in a single volume the most relevant information on the extent and nature of the father's influence.

Books concerning parents and children—particularly those that achieve wide popular appeal—are often constructed of generalizations of unspecified origin. The frequent use of unsubstantiated opinion in these works may be partly responsible for the low regard which many people have for "child-rearing experts." The synthesis of material in the present book is achieved through describing pertinent aspects of the methods and findings of research that has been conducted on the topic. The direct and indirect effects of a father's behavior are not easy to study. I have attempted to select studies that, along with being specifically relevant to the topic, have successfully used adequate research methods and statistical procedures.

The information in this book owes its existence to the hundreds of investigators who have studied this area. Those whose work has seemed particularly significant are John Nash, Miriam Johnson, Henry Biller, and Alfred Heilbrun.

1 current views
of the father

> The man is no longer king in his
> castle; there has been a palace
> revolution and the father has
> emerged as the court jester.
> LeMasters, 1971, p. 23

The word "parent" usually refers to a mother or a father. Some current sources seem to suggest a different usage in which a parent is first and foremost a child's mother, and, peripherally, a child's father.

In both popular magazines and in more scholarly literature, comments about the father's lack of involvement in the family, maternal upstaging of the male sex role, loss of authority, and other belittling evaluations are evident (Nash, 1965). Let us begin by looking at some examples of the slighting of the father's role.

In an article titled "The Father as Non-Parent" (Louisell and Carroll, 1969) the authors describe an abortion statute adopted in California. The statute disregards the interests and rights of the father, even if he is married to the mother who is seeking the abortion. The decision to conduct an abortion is apparently left to the mother and medical personnel. Injunctions sought by

1

husband-fathers have been denied by the courts on the
ground that the father has "no right or standing to object
to an abortion." In contrast to this absence of rights,
several provisions of California law spell out obligations
for support that the father incurs beginning with the
conception of his child, whether or not the parents are
married.

Several authors have pointed out that when "parents" are studied in research programs the fathers are
rarely included.

> In several research reports surveyed by the writer,
> 2,295 mothers were questioned about their parental
> role but not one father was interviewed. This omission
> is even more startling when it is remembered that the
> sampling design of these studies was given elaborate
> consideration by the researchers. (LeMasters, 1971, pp.
> 28-29)

The omission of fathers from studies about parents'
influence on children seems to involve the assumption
either that the father does not play a significant part in
the family, or that the father's attitudes and behavior are
adequately represented by the mother.

Several authors have pointed to the fact that the
mass media often portray the father as if he were the
incompetent Dagwood in the comic strip *Blondie.*

> . . . we see the embattled father struggling to main-
> tain his self-image in the face of an aggressive wife-
> mother and a powerful adolescent peer group. If he
> turns to television for relief, his ego (in the United
> States) will be additionally assaulted by programmes
> [sic] in which women and children consistently outwit
> father, for advertisers slant their programmes in favour
> of women because about 80 percent of family purchases
> are made by the wife-mother. (LeMasters, 1971, p. 27)

In describing the literature on child care and youth

guidance in Germany, Metraux (1955) pointed to a pattern in that country:

> Although the experts formally emphasize the importance of parental unity and of a full family life, the father appears only rather distantly and indistinctly as a co-educator or, in examples of parental misguidance and juvenile difficulty, either as the worried, angry, outraged companion of the mother or as a minor villain who disturbs the peace of the home, who excites, spoils or spanks the darling or the naughty child, who interferes with proper education. (p. 211)

A recent *Redbook* article titled "The One Man No Woman Ever Escapes" (1971) discussed a problem with fathers that was described as "common" in father-daughter relationships. The article reported on group meetings in which several women told a psycho-analytically-oriented psychiatrist of the sexually seductive behavior of their fathers toward them.

An article of similar orientation in a professional journal discusses the father's role in the psychotherapeutic treatment of children. The authors (Rubenstein and Levitt, 1957) describe three categories of fathers of children in treatment, "those marked by outstanding passivity," "mechanical fathers," and "American cowboys." They complain that it is usually mothers who bring the child in to treatment, but it is frequently the father who terminates it.

Another group of comments points to a particular trend in the nature of the father's role, a fading of the masculinity and authority that were characteristic of him in the past. The writers vary in how desirable they find this trend to be.

> Compared to the leonine 19th-century father, today's Pop goes like a weasel—bumbling, plaintive, ignoble and ignored. He is a domesticated, diaper-changing, dish-washing, passive breadwinner. If he

presides anywhere, he does so at the foot of the table. (Levin, 1965, p. 69)

As anthropologist Ashley Montagu recently wrote, "Today, while the titular head of the family may still be the father, everyone knows that he is little more than chairman, at most, of the entertainment committee." The long Atlantic crossing washed away the teaching functions of the traditional European father. The new land had new ways, and he could not teach what he himself did not understand (Blum, 1964, p. 98)

Dr. Benjamin Spock is one of several authors who suggest that loss of authority by some fathers may result from personality defects rather than from efforts to be more democratic.

. . . I consider the most important and frequent cause of the shirking of discipline by fathers in America: the disposition of some men here to be passive and submissive toward their wives and the tendency of a number of women to be too bossy toward husbands. He is a father in name and an adult in years, but he still feels like an immature son in relationship to his motherlike wife. (p. 31)

Other authors suggest that our culture values the paternal role as less than the best kind of masculinity.

Loving almost means being soft. Being gentle and kind almost means being a sissy. A loving and gentle father is consciously or unconsciously looked upon as a psychological failure in the sense that he isn't really a *he*-man. (Bartemeier, 1953, p. 280)

Virile (strong) men on television are either bachelors, widowers, or divorced, and the married men with children (fathers) are portrayed as somewhat ridiculous, incompetent, and confused. Nobody could hate or fear the poor devils—a humane person could only pity them. (LeMasters, 1971, p. 22)

A final complaint about the father concerns his lack of involvement in the family. Part of this complaint refers to the small amount of time spent at home by the father.

> . . . Philip Wylie observed that there are 168 hours in a week. "The average man spends about 40 of them at work. Allow another 15 hours for commuting time, lunch, overtime, etc. Then set aside 56 hours, 8 each night for sleep. That adds up to 111 hours, leaving dad 57 hours he can find time to be a father to his children." Now, how many of these 57 hours does the average father actually spend with his children? Well, one group of 300 7th and 8th grade boys kept accurate records for a two-week period. The average time the father and son had alone together for an entire week was 7½ minutes. Thus, the price of business success or professional achievement might sometimes occur at the expense of being less adequate as a father. (Brown, 1961, p. 702)

One question raised by the study referred to above is, does the father have to be alone together with the child to have an influence? The father's time alone with a child may not be the only time that counts.

Another author criticizes the executive as a father in an article titled "Why Do Executives' Children Run Away?"

> . . . the executive should schedule time to spend with his children and look on it as therapy—just as much as playing golf or getting drunk or shooting skeet with the boys. You can't come home and say to a kid, "Tell me what your problems are and I'll tell my secretary and she'll take care of them." (Margetts, 1968, p. 42)

In addition, it has often been pointed out that our society does little or nothing intentionally to orient males to be fathers, or to prepare them to function in that role.

> One of life's most responsible and significant challenges, namely fatherhood, often involves no training or preparation whatsoever. To drive a car, one must pass certain tests and meet certain criteria that indicate at least minimum competence; however, to become a biological father, no requirements are considered necessary and, generally, none are required. (Brown, 1961, p. 701)

This comment was part of a speech delivered to cadets at the United States Air Force Academy. The speech itself seems like a unique event, since it is rare that a group of males, outside of the medical or behavioral science fields, is addressed on child-related topics. The speaker also pointed out that the Academy is one of few institutions of higher learning that have a required course in marriage and the family. "There is recognition here of the significance of family relations in a man's future life, in this case, his future military life."

Recognition that few fathers have had specific preparation for raising children may be the basis of the assumption implied in a comment by John Bowlby (1952): "In the case of fathers who are left with motherless children, either temporarily while the mother is in the hospital or permanently, the provision of a housekeeper service is much preferable to removing the children."

Some writers discuss the historical factors that have led to the ambiguous status of today's fathers. Gorer (1948), an English cultural anthropologist, who studied American culture, suggests that it is necessary for the American father to lose his authority. He relates this to the education of American children which emphasizes the manner in which American patriots threw off the English authority.

> . . . to reject authority became a praiseworthy and

specifically American act, and the sanctions of society were added to the individual motives for rejecting the family authority personified in the father. . . . But whether the individual father hindered or helped his children to become a different sort of person from what he was, was a question of minor importance; the making of an American demanded that the father should be rejected both as a model and as a source of authority. (p. 31)

The industrial revolution is identified as another factor in partially removing the father from the family in terms of the distance of the father's work from the home, the number of hours he is absent from the home, and the obscurity of his work role in the perception of his children.

Two generations ago, whether the father was farmer, writer, parson, planter, carpenter, ironworker, toolmaker, or storekeeper, the son had a chance to watch him at work and take pride in him. Today, the father on his job and the son at home or at school are separated. The son cannot watch his father at work, let alone help him. The father usually feels he must not bring his plant or office home, or he has no desire to do so. In either case, he doesn't talk about his job at dinner. I have seen young sons who have only the vaguest notion of what their fathers do. (Lerner, 1965, p. 95)

Some writers have quoted the children on this problem.

Deborah, a third grader, was frowning. "Well, according to my father I hardly ever see him. You should make it so children can see your father. Mine works late and he's supposed to be home Sundays, but sometimes he works then too."
Brian turned to Deborah and said, "If a man plays too much with children, you turn poor." (Cohen, 1965, p. 61)

Another writer (O'Gara, 1962) refers to "the boy

reported on in the *New Yorker* cartoon, who answered a question about his father's occupation by saying that he didn't know what his father did all day, but whatever it was it made him sick to the stomach."

These examples represent only part of contemporary opinion on the role of fathers. Some of the other comments and opinions are more benign, while others are even more critical than the examples presented. There is obvious validity in some of the criticism. The main point is that there are more than enough negative comments to raise questions about the significance or desirability of the father's influence on his children. Although far more has been written about mothers than about fathers, there has been enough acceptable research concerning fathers to provide substantial information on the father's influence on his children. The goal of the remainder of this chapter is to examine research findings which have some bearing on the questions suggested by the examples cited. Just as the former examples cited represent negation of the father's significance, the studies in the following portion represent affirmation of some aspect of paternal involvement with, and significance to, the father's children. Other possible goals, such as attempting to compare the relative influence of mothers and fathers in particular areas of development, are not pursued.

A number of studies bear on the question of the degree and nature of the father's involvement with children. One type of study looks at the early and intense involvement of some fathers, beginning before the child is born.

Munroe and Munroe (1971) studied three of the several societies in which males are found to experience pregnancy-like symptoms during their wives' pregnancies. The three groups studied were white men from Boston, Massachusetts; black Caribs in British Honduras; and Logoli in Africa. Such symptoms occurred in 92 percent of the black Carib men who were interviewed, and in around half of the American and Logoli men. The authors reasoned that such symptoms would be more likely to occur in men with some degree of cross-sex identity. They expected to find that the men who experienced symptoms would show feminine responses on covert measures of sex identity, but would show hypermasculine responses on more obvious measures. Several aspects of their findings supported their expectations. In two of the societies the men who showed pregnancy-like symptoms and evidence of cross-sex identity were from homes characterized by absence of the father or other adult males.

Other authors (Wainwright, 1966; Liebenberg, 1967) have described the reactions of fathers to the birth of their children, again focusing on deficits of some fathers who react to this change in their status in maladaptive ways. Some of the fathers studied required hospitalization because of the mental disorders they developed following the births of their children.

Part of an interview that one of the writer's students, Liza Avetissian, conducted with a young married couple illustrates the constructive involvement of a not too unusual father and his influence on the mother:

> Their daughter was born during Amy and John's second year of marriage. They have presently been married four years. Both parents were frightened at the prospect of being parents since John was in school.
> Both sets of in-laws were very encouraging toward the pregnancy and encouraged Amy and John to accept the situation and make the best of it, for the

child's sake. John, who from my observations is more perceptive than his wife, immediately sensed her negative attitudes toward the child in her first months of pregnancy. He immediately began to take an active role in the preparations for the child's birth. After talking to Amy's doctor he persuaded her to attend prenatal classes with him. In this way he felt her fear of having the baby would decrease and her attitude would improve.

Both parents were consistent in attending classes and, because of John's positive attitudes and enthusiasm, Amy also developed a more positive attitude toward the baby.

John was very consistent with Amy concerning her breathing exercises and helped her to watch her diet very carefully. When the baby was born John helped Amy in the delivery room. Amy claims that his presence made the experience of natural childbirth a truly memorable experience. John on the other hand felt that by helping to deliver the baby, the baby really seemed a part of him.

Recent developments in a line of research long-focused on maternal behavior in monkeys seems to show that male monkeys exhibit a natural pattern of caring for infants (Mitchell, Redican, and Gomber, 1974). Initial indications are that the male rhesus monkeys became more attached to infants over time while the attachment of females to infants decreased, the males moved toward threats to the infant while the female withdrew with the infant, and the males showed a pattern of more frequent and intense play with the infant than was shown by the mothers. The investigators pointed to the inadequacy of views picturing the human male as limited in his paternal behavior.

Further constructive involvement of fathers is described in a study of forty-five families with infants (Pedersen and Robson, 1969). The fathers were a somewhat select group since they averaged three years of college education. Of interest are the data obtained from a detailed inquiry of the mothers regarding how the fathers spent their time with the babies. The mothers estimated that the fathers had a mean of twenty-six hours a week in the house during the babies' waking hours. They spent an average of about eight hours playing with the baby, with different fathers spending from forty-five minutes to twenty-six hours. The play time did not differ with the sex of the babies. There was evidence that the way the fathers behaved with these eight- to nine-and-one-half-month-old children already influenced their attachments to the fathers, as indicated by "directed smiles, vocalizations, increased motor activity, and a general level of excitement upon seeing the father after some period of absence."

The fathers whose male children showed relatively clear attachment were "nurturant, actively but patiently involved with the baby, and more emotionally interested in his upbringing and development." The authors point to this pattern of behavior as matching the conditions which facilitate the child's identification with the father. The authors speculate that the fathers who were most actively involved in nurturant and child-centered behaviors are representative of an increasing trend.

A couple of studies done in the 1940's found evidence of substantial father involvement with children at that point in time. Gardner (1943) reported on 300 interviews which were focused on the fathers' evaluation of their paternal duties with their 874 children. Ninety-nine percent of the fathers said they wanted children. However, it may have been a bit late to ask them that question. Eighty-six percent said that children made their marriages happier. An interesting reason for having children cited by 21 percent of the fathers was that they thought children satisfied a natural desire. On the other hand one father wanted children for their work capacity.

In describing their activities in bringing up the children, 60 percent of the fathers cited various routine activities they performed or gave "plenty" of care. In some examples of specific activities of fathers (at various ages of their children) 63 percent gave help on home-work, 37 percent gave sex instruction, and 80 percent assigned children some of an identified 516 duties or tasks. Degree of involvement with the children seemed to vary widely even between men in the same occupation. Companionship and affection, direct or indirect teaching of ideals, and nature of discipline and training were viewed as the more important areas of their duties, judging from the behaviors the fathers described as their strong points or weak points. Provision for material welfare, which is viewed by some authors as the father's main function, received little emphasis by these fathers in the interviews.

In a subsequent study Gardner (1947) studied fathers from the viewpoint of their children. On a forty-five-item questionnaire, 388 fifth- and sixth-graders described their fathers in ways that support Gardner's earlier findings concerning the degree of the father's involvement, but add some additional considerations. About forty percent of the children described their fathers as playing with them every day, while about 35 percent said their fathers played with them weekends or once in a while. Eighty-one percent thought their fathers liked to play with them. The children specified 372 different recreational activities the fathers engaged in with them, along with 393 different chores the father assigned to them. For most services the children tended to go to their mothers, but fathers were contacted for broken toys (70%) and money (58%). There were roughly twice as many children who liked the mother a little better than the father, as compared to those who preferred the father to the mother. Things the fathers did that the children wished they would not do included swearing and smoking cigars, while the children wanted higher frequencies of giving an allowance or money, allowing more play, allowing more shows, and more talking to the child.

Tasch (1952) interviewed eighty-five New York City fathers of diverse nationality, religion, occupation, and educational level. They had eighty male and eighty female children. The order in which the fathers stressed the importance of different aspects of their roles with their children was companion, economic provider, guide and teacher, child rearer, authority, developer of personal characteristics and habits, and maintainer of family unity.

High percentages of the fathers reported involvement in such child rearing activities as routine daily care and safety (94.1%); development of motor abilities, acquisition of skills, interests (87%); development of intellectual abilities and interests (87%); going to places of recreation (80%); and development of social standards, conduct, and control (74.1%). It is interesting to note that these activities are those that some traditional writers would class as instrumental or masculine, since they are largely oriented toward success in the world outside of the family. Smaller percentages of fathers reported involvement in such areas as emotional development (41.2%); moral and spiritual development (38.8%); maintaining family unity (37.6%); and development of personality characteristics (30.6%). These activities are frequently described as more expressive or feminine because of their personal or family emphasis. Material to be examined later in this book will indicate that fathers do affect these areas of development as well, whether or not they are aware of it.

Similar observations regarding which aspects of child development fathers regard as pertinent to themselves were made by personnel of a child guidance clinic serving rural northern Alberta (Davidson and Schrag, 1968). They found that in 31 percent of their cases both parents attended the clinic, in 51 percent only the mother attended, in 8 percent only the father attended, and in 10 percent neither parent attended. Fathers came to the clinic more often if it was held at the school rather than the public health office, if the parents considered the problem to be an educational problem rather than a conduct problem, and if the teacher was directly interested or involved. Emphasis on the child's educational progress, so important for the child's eventual success outside the family, seemed to be the key to involving the fathers.

Returning to the Tasch study, in disciplining children about 64 percent of the fathers said both parents took responsibility, while 28 percent said the mother was the main disciplinarian, and 8 percent said they were the main disciplinarian.

The activities of the fathers with their children differed in number and nature depending on the age of the child, with the greatest number of activities occurring in the middle years of childhood. The average of 8.6 activities with 0 to 4 year olds focused on feeding, bathing, and similar activities. The 11.7 activities with 5 to 8 year olds focused more on intellectual communication and instruction in social interaction. For the 9 to 12 year olds the 12.2 activities included those of the preceding period with an increased focus on chores, allowances, and other aspects of "work and responsibility." The 7.8 activities with 13 to 14 year olds included more "companionable" activities such as going to the movies, ball-games, and other types of recreation. The 3.1 activities with the children of 17 or older stress companionable and "togetherness" aspects.

Tasch noted that although the nature of chores assigned, physical contacts, and motor activities clearly differed with the sex of the child, the fathers showed little awareness of their significance as examples of masculinity or of the sex-typing effect of their activities.

While the studies by Gardner and by Tasch were conducted some time ago, it is reasonable to expect that their findings with regard to the father's involvement in child rearing are conservative indications of present levels of involvement. Many contemporary observers suggest that today's fathers are becoming more involved in child rearing as the traditional dichotomy between male and female parental roles in the family weakens.

From interviews with 379 mothers of kindergarten children, Sears, Maccoby, and Levin (1957) found that fathers tended to participate more in the rearing of the first child than with subsequent ones. The oldest child of either sex, or the male only child, was the child with whom fathers were most involved in discipline. The mothers noted that the father's punishment seemed more effective than the mother's, perhaps because it had more novelty since the father was with the child less.

Evidence on the validity of the frequent procedure of studying only mothers to find out about both parents is provided in a study of sixty third-graders and most of their 120 parents (Eron, Banta, Walder, and Laulicht, 1961). The boys and girls were selected from a larger group on the basis of high, medium, or low levels of aggression. The parents were then interviewed individually. Mothers and fathers were found not to agree about their children in rating either the children's behavior or interactions with other children. When comparing the parents' responses with other, independent ratings of the children's behavior, the fathers' ratings often corresponded more closely to the independent ratings than did the mothers' ratings. Thus, it is possible that in studying only the mothers the researchers have sometimes obtained the less valid of two more or less different parental views.

Reports of the fathers' psychological involvement with childbirth were referred to earlier. It is also appropriate to mention two articles which reflect the father's involvement near the end of childhood. Van Manen (1968) was interested in the father's influence on the socialization of adolescents, stating, "The father, par excellence the representative of the outside world, is hypothetically the person who could wield special influence at this time" (p. 143). Data were collected from a longitudinal study of the parents of 325 children. The adolescent's agreement with his parents on what values were important for him to adopt was highly correlated (Phi = .94) with the father's "effectiveness." The father "effectiveness" rating was based on sixteen aspects of job satisfaction, such as chances for advancement and overall satisfaction with standard of living. The father's "affectiveness" rating (understanding, affection, etc.) was highly correlated (Phi = .83) with adolescent value agreement, as was the affectiveness of the mother (Phi = .79). In earlier childhood the mother's affective role seemed to have a decidedly greater relationship to the child's socialization than did that of the father, but this apparently changed by adolescence, with the father coming to have an equal significance.

Deutscher (1968) talks about the influence, upon the child who is beginning school, of seeing the father separate from the family and go off to work each day. While the child may not clearly understand the father's work, he may well be learning from the father as a model in terms of whether the father presents the outside world as inviting or threatening, whether he seems satisfied with his position and status, and how the rest of the family evaluates the father's providing. Deutscher goes on to relate the father's example to the eventual work choices of the child in young adulthood.

> Studies agree on many of the biographical background factors of productive people in the arts, sciences, and the professions. Preponderantly, they have had well-working fathers, often in the professions, and come from homes where positive values have been placed on learning and achievement. The father is not necessarily totally accepting, loving or involved; the nature of his force as a model refers to his competence in his own work in an effective context of prestige, status, satisfaction, and achievement. (p. 884)

Incidentally, Colfax and Allen (1967) found that children at the sixth grade or high school levels showed an upward bias in locating their father's occupation on a precoded list. Fathers with blue-collar occupations were often boosted upward to white-collar categories.

Summary

This chapter has introduced a few of the many articles which provide evidence concerning the father's influence on his children's development, and has also introduced some of the more critical comments in the literature.

While some comments describe fathers as uninvolved, there is evidence suggesting that the typical father is more likely to be regularly involved in a wide range of activities with his children, activities with a variety of implications for the developmental process. Evidence is available that omission of the father from many of the past studies of "parents" may have resulted in missing a different and sometimes more valid view of the child's development. Some comments may reflect changes away from past sex role dichotomies, changes that may encourage more participation of modern fathers in their children's development.

Some aspects of criticism of the role taken by the father appear justified, but there is much that indicates significant aspects of the same role. Subsequent chapters of this book examine the father's influence on his children by focusing on several distinct areas of influence. The chapter on father-absence deals with studies which assess the influence of fathers by examination of the effects of his absence. The chapters on paternal influence on the development of daughters and sons cover the unique aspects of paternal impact on female or male children.

The fifth chapter reviews the influence of the father in the development of several characteristics which develop similarly in children of either sex. The final chapter discusses the amount of influence due to fathers and the ideal pattern of behavior for fathers.

2 father-
absence effects

One method of exploring the significance of the father in a family is the negative approach of looking at the effects of his absence. Comparisons between characteristics of children from intact families and children from families in which the father has been absent for a significant period of time are common. The differences that are found between children of intact families and those of father-absent families are grouped in this chapter under the headings of characteristics of personality and social behavior, masculinity or femininity, cognitive development, and attitudes toward parents.

Differences that are found between children of families with or without fathers offer rather inconclusive evidence of the fathers' effects on the children. The absence of the father is frequently not the only variable between the two types of families. The father-absent family may well have a lower average income, less time when the mother can be with the children, and other characteristics related only indirectly to the father's absence. Little of the research is well enough controlled to demonstrate conclusively that it is the absence of the father *per se* which causes the noted differences between families.

A number of studies described near the end of this chapter describe other characteristics of the family which can modify the effects of father-absence on a child. These characteristics include the child's age, the age and sex of his siblings, the socioeconomic status of the family, and the pattern of behavior that the mother follows in her husband's absence.

With some reservations then, let us examine some of the research findings that are available.

The relationship of father-absence
to the child's personality and social behavior

A focus on the relationship between father-absence and various characteristics of the personality and social behavior of the child has characterized the largest category of studies. A number of the studies coincided with World War II and made use of the absence of fathers for military service. A couple of these studies assume that children will project their own characteristics into an ambiguous situation (Sears, Pintler, and Sears, 1946; Sears, 1951). The investigators observed and rated aggression of the children as they played with dolls representing a family of five members. Approximately half of the children were from homes in which the father was consistently present, and the others were from father-absent homes. They found boys and girls from father-absent homes to be more like each other in aggressiveness than were boys and girls from normal homes. This finding suggests that the sex-role development of the children from father-absent homes may have been affected, since higher aggressiveness in boys seems to be one of the main personality characteristics that distinguish boys from girls in father-present families.

Another study compared children whose fathers had been absent for military service during their early childhood with younger children in the same families who had had the father consistently present (Seplin, 1952). The older children were described as more "deeply disturbed" and closer to their mothers. (Because of the procedure used the results of this study might be attributed to differences in the relative position in the family of older and younger children.)

One report described examination of father-absence effects in data from a long term study of boys from an underprivileged background (McCord, McCord, and Thurber, 1962). Some of the boys were selected for the study because it was thought likely that they would become delinquent. Father-absence in these families was generally due to divorce, separation, or death. As in the studies mentioned above, the authors rated the aggressiveness of the boys from father-absent homes as less typically masculine. The authors believed that the sexual anxiety they observed in some of the father-absent boys could be a response to a generally unstable environment rather than paternal absence alone. Of particular interest is the fact that they found more gang related delinquency among boys from unbroken homes with quarreling parents than among boys from father-absent homes. Such a finding complicates the practical question of whether or not a couple in distress should "stay together for the children's sake."

Anderson (1968) reported a strong association between father-absence in the background of boys and higher delinquency rates, with this association not occurring in cases of mother-absence. He noted, however, that in cases of mother-absence, surrogate mothers, such as an older female consistently in the home, were present much more often than father surrogates were present in father-absent homes.

In this clinical study of 143 training school and

control group boys, it appeared that the presence of a father substitute was most helpful when the boy was between four and seven years of age for deterring later delinquency. There were also cases of father-present boys who wound up in the training school, and cases of father-absent boys who did not. In the former group Anderson observed that, out of thirteen fathers, three had serious medical conditions which limited their roles in the family, two worked nights and overtime, and six were heavy drinkers. The effect of these fathers who were present was described as excessively passive or excessively chiding and punitive. The thirteen boys who had never been arrested and had absent fathers had, with one exception, been separated from their natural fathers since early childhood or infancy, and in most cases the natural father or a surrogate had been present later in childhood.

Father-absence has been a factor commonly included in studies of the causes of juvenile delinquency. In his study of 44,448 cases in Philadelphia, Monahan (1957) notes, "For white boys the percentage of all cases in the recidivist class increases from 32 where both parents are married and living together to 38 where the father is dead and the boy is with his mother, to 42 where both parents are dead and the child is with a surrogate family, to 46 where the parents are living apart and the child is with the mother, to 49 where the parents are divorced, to 55 where the boy is living with his unmarried mother" (p. 257). He noted similar patterns for white girls, and for black children of both sexes. While rates of father-absence are found to be as much as twice as high in the families of delinquents as they are in the families of nondelinquents (Glueck & Glueck, 1968), in the context of the many variables influencing delinquency, father-absence *per se* appears less crucial than the socioeconomic status of the family (which, of course, reflects one or both parents' occupations), characteristics of the neighborhood and community, the nature of maternal supervision, and the "climate" of the home (Herzog & Sudia, 1970).

Looking at another indication of severe maladjustment, loss of the father or the mother during childhood seems to be related to an increased risk of later suicidal behavior in the child (Dorpat, Jackson, & Ripley, 1965). In a study of 114 successful suicides and 121 consecutive suicide attempts, 50 percent of the former and 63.9 percent of the latter individuals had lost parents in childhood, mostly through death, the child leaving home before age 18, or divorce. In an analysis of 199 of the completed or attempted suicide cases, 67 individuals had lost both parents, 27 had lost only the father, and 18 had lost only the mother. Loss of the parent through death was particularly closely linked with serious suicidal efforts.

Trunnell (1968) studied psychiatric outpatient records of 107 father-absent and 50 father-present children. The objectivity or reliability of his analysis is not clear from his report. On the basis of his previous work he hypothesized that the "psychopathology" of the father-absent child would be greater with (1) greater developmental problems of the child prior to the father's absence, (2) more severe personality disturbance in the mother, (3) the child's more unsatisfactory relationship with the father, (4) fewer male substitutes available, and (5) earlier and longer absence of the father. The author hypothesized that paternal absence is never the sole cause of abnormal development. In looking at the relationship between nine stress factors such as those above, and whether the father-absent child was classified as more or less severely disturbed, the presence of only one factor was characteristic in slightly over half of the less severely disturbed group, while the presence of three, four, or more factors was characteristic of practically all of the twenty-nine severely disturbed children. From these results one would not expect a child without a father to show severe disturbance if the conditions were that the loss of the father occurred before the child was three, the child had not shown signs of any developmental deviance previously, the mother was fairly well adjusted, there was a remarriage by the mother, etc. On the other hand if several such factors fell in a less optimal direction, the chances of the child being severely disturbed increase. One could add that this sort of pattern might be expected to hold true whether or not father absence is involved.

Among the father-absence studies with a unique setting is that of the success of Peace Corps volunteers overseas (Suedfeld, 1967). The author selected at random thirty-five files of volunteers of both sexes who were nearing successful completion of their two-year tour, and thirty-four files of those who had returned to the United States prior to the scheduled completion of their tours because of problems of "adjustment and conduct (including psychiatric termination)." Forty-four percent of the unsuccessful volunteers were from father-absent homes (father absent for any reason for at least five years before the volunteers' fifth birthday) as opposed to only nine percent of father-absence in the histories of the successful volunteers. The author drew a second sample of fifty-five files and again found a forty-four percent incidence of father-absence in the unsuccessful volunteers compared to fourteen percent for the successful volunteers. The results were not highly likely to be due to socioeconomic status differences since nearly all of the volunteers were college graduates. Absence of the mother, family size, birth order, and the volunteer's sex were other family variables examined in the study, but these apparently did not differentiate significantly between the successful and unsuccessful volunteers.

A similar study of 272 male volunteers for the Royal Danish Army was conducted by Hjelholt (1958). Recalling Parsons' view that the father's role influences the child's adaptation to the world outside the family, the study examined the effect of broken homes (which usually means absence of the father) on failure of these young men to complete their initial military training because of "maladjustment." Those failing to complete the course included a significantly greater number of men from broken homes than was true for those who did succeed. It was found, as expected, that before the age of five loss of the mother had more effect, while after five loss of the father had more effect.

From these studies we get additional gross indications that the presence or absence of the father is related to the adequacy of the child's later adjustment in varied situations. A similar conclusion can be drawn from a study of fifty black unwed mothers in Chicago (Barglow, et al., 1968). These girls were eleven to sixteen years old, from poverty backgrounds, and of an average eighth-grade level of education. The authors compared twenty-five girls, who became pregnant again within an average of twelve months of the delivery of their first child, to twenty-five who had not become pregnant by the same time. The authors noted a 78 percent rate of father absence in their twice-pregnant groups, 39 percent in their once-pregnant groups, and a rate of 25 percent among comparable families of nonpregnant girls in the

Chicago area. Studies of unmarried mothers have obtained variable results, however, with the significance of broken homes appearing different with different samples of subjects (Vincent, 1961).

A different type of approach is utilized by Pedersen (1966), who compared a group of 27 boys who had emotional and behavioral problems with a group of 30 normal boys. The boys were 11 to 15 year old military dependents. The two groups were equivalent on several aspects of the father's military status, the age of the parents, and the boy's age and sibling position. In both groups the fathers had been absent an average of seventeen months, and the author's approach was to look at the correlation between the length of a particular father's absence and his son's maladjustment as measured by the Rogers Test of Personality Adjustment. It was found that these two variables were moderately correlated in the disturbed group ($r = .53$, $p = .01$), but were not correlated in the normal group. In other words the length of the father's absence was related to maladjustment only in the disturbed group. The parents had each filled out a Minnesota Multiphasic Personality Inventory for the experimenter, and it was found that the mothers of the disturbed group were more poorly adjusted on five of the subscales (Hs, P, Hy, Pa, Sc). This difference in adjustment between the two groups did not hold true for fathers. Thus Pedersen apparently found that in two very similar groups of children, whose fathers had been gone for similar lengths of time and at similar ages of the children, one group had mothers who were more maladjusted and the children became more disturbed the more the father was gone, while the other group had better adjusted mothers and the adjustment of the children was not affected by the length of absence of the father.

Santrock (1970) presented some evidence that the type of personality characteristics related to father-absence may depend on the child's age when the father's absence begins. Father-absence was due to divorce, separation, desertion, or death. The author used teacher ratings of the characteristics of 45 fifth-grade males. He obtained some evidence that boys whose fathers had been absent from the birth to two-year-old period showed more shame, guilt, inferiority, and less trust than was true for boys whose father-absence began later. This had been expected from reasoning based on Erik Erikson's conception of early developmental stages.

Hoffman (1971) looked at the effects of father-absence on conscience development in 497 seventh-grade white children; 25 of the boys and 28 of the girls had had no adult male in their home during the six-month period preceding the study. A control group of father-present children matched on intelligence, social class and family size was chosen from the larger pool of children. Hoffman used the children's semiprojective story-completion tasks, judgment of hypothetical transgressions, judgment of the importance of personal attributes, and teachers' ratings to assess the morality of the children. On six of the eight indexes used, the father-absent boys obtained significantly different scores from those of the father-present boys. The father-absent boys had lower scores on maximum guilt, internal moral judgment, acceptance of blame, moral values, conformity to rules, and higher scores on overt aggression. There were no significant differences for girls. Hoffman reasoned that it was the absence of a paternal model that led to the detrimental effect of father-absence for boys. As a check on this he was able to compare a group of father-present boys who had very high scores on a measure of identification with their father to a group that had very low scores. Weaker identification with the paternal model had similar but less severe effects than was true for the absence of the paternal model. The same reasoning would explain why girls would be less affected by father-absence, as they would be expected to have closer identification with the mother.

Hoffman also pointed out that absence of a readily available paternal model was probably not the only effect of father-absence. In data obtained from the children concerning the mother's discipline and affection, the author found that in the father-absent families the mothers expressed affection less frequently toward the boys, and more frequently toward the girls, than was the case for the father-present families. The author speculated that the mothers may attempt to compensate for the father's absence by being more affectionate, but that it may be more difficult to do this with boys because of their "more abrasive qualities" and/or because they may receive some of the mother's remaining resentment toward the husband in those cases where father-absence resulted from a divorce.

Hoffman also discusses the inconsistent findings (evident in the survey of studies in this chapter as well) regarding the effect of father-absence on the level of aggressiveness in boys. In studies using measures of fantasy aggression such as the doll-play technique, aggression has been found to be lower for father-absent boys, while it has been found to be higher in studies using measures of overt aggression. Hoffman suggests that the father-absent boy is less likely to develop effective control over his behavior and is more likely to express overt aggression; however, he then has less need to express aggression in fantasy. Unfortunately the findings regarding aggression cited in this chapter involve more inconsistencies than just that between fantasy and overt behavioral measures.

The relationship of father-absence to masculinity or femininity in children

One variable of the child's development which appears in most considerations of the father's impact on the family is that of the child's relative masculinity or femininity. This variable turns out to be related to many aspects of personality and social development in general. The child's behavior in such areas as aggression, achievement motivation, and dependency helps to determine how masculine or feminine the child is considered to be. The importance of masculinity-femininity as influenced by father is significant in the area of father absence as well.

Barclay and Cusumano (1967) examined the possibility that boys from father-absent homes may adopt the sex-role orientation of the mother and then have difficulty in achieving adequate masculine identification. The authors mention some articles indicating that such a male may defensively deny having any feminine characteristics. However, feminine characteristics which are not easily spotted as such are less likely to be denied. Forty male adolescents were studied, half of them being from father-absent homes (father and father surrogates absent since the child was five) and half from father-present homes. Half of each of these two groups were composed of white boys and half of black, resulting in four groups of ten persons each. These groups were selected from a larger sample so that the average age, academic grade-point average, intelligence quotient, and socioeconomic status were comparable. This type of procedure controls some of the differences between the groups, other than father-absence and race, that might account for the results of the study. As mentioned above, father-absent families might be expected to have lower incomes and this factor in itself could result in some differences between children from father-absent and father-present families. However, when the experimenter has selected subjects of similar socioeconomic status to assign to the different groups, any differences found are then more likely to be directly related to the variable being examined.

The measurements used to provide the father-absent boys with an opportunity to deny feminine characteristics were the Gough Femininity Scale from the California Psychological Inventory and the subject's ratings of his father, mother, and self between a series of bipolar adjectives (semantic differential). The measure which was of less evident relevance to masculinity-femininity was the rod and frame test. As predicted from the reasoning of the authors the boys from father-absent homes were more field-dependent on the rod and frame test, and females were generally more field-dependent than males on this task. They also found that the black groups were more field-dependent than the whites. Differences in masculinity were not found on the two more obvious measures which were administered to the subjects.

An article by Burton and Whiting (1961) also provides a theoretical discussion of the effect of father-absence on the development of masculinity in males. They describe the child as envying the privileges and resources of his parents. This "status envy" results in the child practicing, either in play or in fantasy, the role behaviors that go with the desired status. The authors describe some evidence from other research that the boy who is raised in a female-centered home in a lower social-class neighborhood may primarily envy the status of females until the time that he begins to associate with an adolescent male gang, particularly if the father is absent. The conflict of sexual identity which follows from the long duration of his envy of the status of females may be responsible for the denial and rejection of anything even remotely feminine that is sometimes observed in delinquent gangs.

This possibility that a boy from a father-absent family might show an over-emphasis of masculine characteristics is included in a study by Hetherington (1966). She reasoned that the age at which separation from the father occurs could differentially affect the pattern of sex-role identification. Early separation could prevent masculine identification from occurring and could create a disruptive effect on learning masculine sex-role behaviors. Later separation might have little effect, or could result in an over-emphasis on masculine behavior that was learned through identification with the father prior to his absence. The dividing point between "early" and "later" separation is usually regarded as roughly five years of age, both in theoretical discussions of sex-role development, and in a sizable number of studies which have explored the knowledge of children of various ages about the appropriateness of various kinds of behavior for males or females in general, or for the child himself.

Hetherington included thirty-two black and thirty-two white boys from a lower socioeconomic status area, all of whom were between nine and twelve years of age and the first born in their family. Half of each group of boys were from father-absent homes and half from father-present homes. The reason for setting up the study so that it would be possible to compare races was that the lower socioeconomic status black family is described as frequently mother-dominated, and it seemed possible that in such families the presence or absence of the father might have less effect on sex-typing in boys. In half of each racial group, separation of the father had occurred at age four or earlier, and in the other half it occurred at age six or later. The causes of father-separation specified were desertion, divorce, death, and illegitimacy.

The boys were all participants at a recreation center, so their behavior was rated on twenty-three scales by recreation directors who had known the boys for at least six months. The boys were also tested individually on the IT Scale for Children (ITSC), which has been used in some of the previous research on sex-role preference in children.

While there was no difference related to father-presence or absence in the ratings for dependence on adults, the boys from father-absent homes were rated as significantly more dependent on peers. In ratings of aggression, boys from father-present homes and those who were separated from their fathers after age six were significantly more aggressive than those who were separated from their fathers earlier. Since dependency and aggression are found to be somewhat more characteristic of females and males respectively (Sears, Rau, and Alpert, 1965) the results do support the expectation of more typically masculine behavior in the boys with later separation from their fathers. The same group and the boys from unbroken homes were also found to have more masculine sex-role preferences than did the early-separated boys. In addition, it was found that the early-separated boys play fewer physical games involving contact (boxing, football, etc.) than do the late-separated or father-present boys. The early-separated boys spend more time in nonphysical, noncompetitive activities (reading, working on puzzles, etc.) than boys from unbroken homes do. The only difference found between racial groups was that the black boys selected more of the physical skill games involving contact. In general then, Hetherington's study does indicate that the boys who were separated from their fathers at the age of four or earlier were less masculine in some areas of their behavior, while boys who were separated after age six are more similar to those from unbroken homes. No particular evidence that the later-separated boy over-emphasizes masculine behavior was mentioned.

Biller has conducted a couple of studies which relate closely to the study by Hetherington. In one of these (1968) he studied twenty-nine boys of lower socioeconomic status and averaging about six and one-half years of age. They were about equally divided into four groups of father-present or absent, race-black or white, composition. The father-absent boys had been without their fathers for at least two years, and in some cases since birth. As in the study by Barclay and Cusumano described earlier in this chapter, Biller focuses on differences in masculinity expressed by the boys depending on whether the measure is at an obvious or less obvious level. As a less than obvious measure each boy was tested individually on the IT Scale for Children (ITSC). In this test the child is shown a figure called "IT" which is of indefinite sex. He is then shown pictures of objects and activities and is asked to pick those "IT" would like. It is assumed the child will follow his own masculine or feminine interests in making the selections. For a more obvious measure the boys were questioned about their own toy, game, and occupational preferences, and were asked to tell which items were masculine and which were feminine in the pictures of the ITSC. The boys were also rated by their classroom teachers on a fifteen-item scale designed to assess overt masculinity.

On the more obvious measures there were no significant differences between father-present and father-absent boys, or between racial groups. On the ITSC significant differences did occur. White father-present boys obtained the most masculine score, black father-absent boys obtained the least masculine score, and the white father-absent and black father-present boys obtained similar scores that fell between the two extreme groups. The author's explanation for the rankings of these four groups is the same as that of Hetherington. It may be noted that the ratings of the boys' overt behavior differed between groups in Hetherington's study while they did not in Biller's. A possible explanation for this discrepancy is that the differences in behavior were more evident in activities typical of the recreation center in the former study, than they would be in the classroom of the latter study where somewhat more uniformity of behavior is imposed. One reason for having some reservations about Biller's findings is that the differential tendency of the groups to pick masculine or feminine activities for "IT" could relate to differences in reaction to this type of projective technique independent of the sex-role orientation of the boy. However, the finding is consistent with that of Barclay and Cusumano (above).

Another of Biller's studies (1969) is similar but somewhat more elaborate. He matched seventeen father-absent five-year-old boys with seventeen father-present boys so that they were similar or identical on socioeconomic status, age, IQ, and sibling distribution.

The boys were kindergarteners of working-class and lower-middle-class backgrounds. They were tested individually on the ITSC as a measure of sex-role *orienta-*

tion. To assess sex-role *preference* the boys were tested on a game preference task in which they were asked to choose which game they would like to play in each of sixteen pairings of a masculine (e.g., football) with a feminine game (e.g., jump rope). Each boy was rated by his teacher on assertiveness, aggressiveness, competitiveness, independence, activity directed toward physical prowess and mastery of the environment, passivity, dependency, and timidity. This rating scale was intended to measure sex-role *adoption.* The effort to measure sex-role learning at the three different levels, (orientation, preference, and adoption), reflects one conception of the development of sex-role behavior. As Biller (1970) describes it:

> Sex-role orientation (or sex-role identification) is considered to be one dimension of an individual's self-concept. It refers to the individual's conscious and/or unconscious perception and evaluation of his maleness and/or femaleness. Sex-role preference relates to the individual's preferential set toward culturally defined representation of sex role. Sex-role adoption pertains to the masculinity and/or femininity of the individual's behavior in social and environmental interactions. (p. 184)

Sex-role orientation is learned before preference or adoption and is more covert. It is the most likely area to be affected by early father absence. Sex-role preference and adoption could be influenced later in the boy's development by influences such as the mother's degree of encouragement of masculine behavior.

The mothers answered a multiple-choice questionnaire concerning the degree to which they encouraged masculine behavior in their sons. In the questionnaire the mother was asked to choose which four alternative responses she would make to such situations as her boy wrestling with another boy, climbing a tree, falling off his tricycle, and others.

The author found that the boys from father-present homes had more masculine ITSC scores, and slightly more masculine game preference scores. The ITSC scores for the boys whose fathers had been absent two or more years indicated lower masculinity than was found for the boys whose fathers had been absent less than that. In examining the mothers' scores on encouragement of masculine behavior, it was found that mothers of father-present boys were slightly more encouraging of masculine behavior. The mothers of father-present boys were more accepting of masculine behavior in their sons, while the mothers of father-absent boys were more ambivalent. The father-absent boys' masculinity scores on the game preference measure and on the teachers' ratings were significantly correlated with the degree of maternal encouragement of masculine behavior shown by their mothers. This relationship did not hold true for ITSC scores, nor were any of these relationships significant for father-present boys.

A study by Stephens (1961) is relevant to this topic, although the procedure does not inspire trust in the results. In a meeting of over thirty social workers the author asked them to consider and compare boys who had little contact with a man living in the home during the first six years of their lives, with boys of similar age, social class, etc., from whole families. Then the social workers were asked to answer eight questionnaire items about the families. Their answers indicated that they did regard the boys from father-absent homes as more feminine. They also thought the mothers in those homes were more jealous of their sons' girl friends than were the mothers in unbroken homes. The author reasoned that the mother's jealousy is related to the Oedipal conflict and the mother being more seductive toward her son because of her sexual continence. Such speculation is, of course, extremely tenuous when based on research with practically no controls.

The relationship of father-absence to intellectual and academic performance of children

The fact that absence of the male parent can be related to his children's cognitive ability would probably serve as a good illustration of how complex the developmental process of human beings is. Surely the vast group of parents that dismiss the task of "raising" children as a simple matter of common sense do not imagine the possibility that the father's role is related to whether his children are higher in verbal or mathematical ability.

Perhaps the earliest study to illustrate a relationship in this area was a 1930 study by Sutherland. The study was primarily focused on the inverse relationship that several studies had shown between the size of children's IQ and the size of their family of origin. The author added the variable of father presence or absence to the study. The first comparison involved 123 father-absent and 116 father-present children from the same schools and classes in Scotland. Those without fathers had been fatherless from birth. The two groups were matched closely on the number of male and female siblings in their families. A similar comparison was made with 724 father-absent and 581 father-present children in England. All were between eleven and fourteen years of age. In both comparisons it was found that brighter children tended to come from smaller families, and that the father-absent children had an average IQ about five points

below that of children from families with the father
present. The explanation mentioned for the effect of
family size is that brighter couples tend to have smaller
families. Because of the hereditary influence their children would tend to be brighter than those from larger
families. No explanation for the effect of father absence is
offered in this study.

Another British study (Maxwell, 1961) compared 292
8 to 13 year old neurotic children with the norms of
British and American children on the Wechsler Intelligence Scale for Children (WISC). The scores of the
neurotic sample were significantly lower on five (for
boys) or six (for girls) of the ten parts of the test which are
usually administered in Britain. In exploring the relationship between seven aspects of the neurotic children's
background and their performance on the test, the author
found absence of the father after the age of five was
significantly related to lower scores on the comprehen-
sion, picture completion, and coding subtests. A similar
relationship below an acceptable level of statistical significance was found with the vocabulary and picture
arrangement subtests. Absence of the father before the
age of five was not significantly related to test performance.

The effect of father-absence on WISC performance
has also been examined with 433 American children
manifesting personality and behavior problems (Lessing,
Zagorin, & Nelson, 1970). The age ranges for the children
ran one to two years older than was true in the British
study. For the 138 children who had had fathers absent
for two or more years the scores for performance IQ,
block design, and object assembly were lower than those
of father-present subjects. Father-absent boys also had
lower scores on the arithmetic subtest. Father-absent

subjects from the working class also obtained lower verbal IQ and full-scale IQ scores. However, middle class father-absent children tended to have higher verbal IQ scores than those of father-present children. Children with prolonged father-absence who now had a stepfather in the home had test scores that did not differ significantly from the scores of father-present subjects.

The authors explored two possible explanations for the influence of father-absence on children's intellectual performance. One hypothesis is that identification with the father facilitates the acquisition of quantitative and spatial-perceptual skills, which are typically male aptitudes. This would explain the somewhat consistent pattern of types of tasks that seem to be affected by father-absence, as well as the more evident effect on males. The second hypothesis was that the development of the same quantitative skills is more vulnerable to stress or "tension interference" resulting from the less optimal home conditions associated directly or indirectly with father-absence.

Carlsmith (1964) refers to the large number of studies that find females tend to be superior to males in verbal aptitude and inferior in quantitative aptitude. He suggests that aptitude patterns are a useful, non-obvious measure of primary sex-role orientation. He notes that the verbal and mathematical scores from the Scholastic Aptitude Test administered to high school juniors and seniors follow the expected pattern of sex differences. He used subjects whose fathers had been absent up to three years for overseas service during World War II to compare with similar but father-present subjects. In comparing twenty pairs of Harvard freshmen matched on father's occupation, education, etc., he found that 13 of the 20 father-absent subjects had verbal scores greater than their math scores, while in the father-present group 18 of the 20 had the usual male pattern of math scores greater than verbal. In studying 272 male and female high school seniors he found similar effects of father absence. Absence of the father in these two samples was before the age of five years and it did relate to test performance while no effect was noted for absence of the father before age five in the preceding study. This discrepancy could be due to the different tests that were used or any of a number of other differences that are apparent between the studies.

A subsequent study adds to Carlsmith's approach by looking at the influence of different patterns of siblings on the American College Entrance Examination (ACE) scores of 295 college students whose fathers had been absent two or more consecutive years, and the scores of 760 father-present students (Sutton-Smith, Rosenberg, and Landy, 1968). The students whose fathers had been absent scored lower on the quantitative, linguistic, and total scores. This finding was most consistent for males. The authors examined the effects of the length of the father's absence, and the child's age at the time of the absence on the test scores. The length of the absence was not significantly related to test scores, but, at least for female students, the child's age at the time of the father's absence was related. The 0-4 and 5-9 year-old age ranges appeared to be the ones during which absence of the father had more effect, but the authors voiced some reservations about this indication.

Looking at the role of family structure, it was found that the effects were stronger in three-child families, moderate in two-child families, and minimal in one-child families. Surprisingly, in the one-child families, a lone daughter was more affected by father absence than a lone son. In looking at two-child families, it was found that children with an opposite sex sibling were more affected by father absence than those with a same sex sibling. The authors offered some tentative speculation that the effects noted in one-child families are related to the child's modeling after the opposite-sexed parent. The only child who is a daughter is affected more by the father's absence (see Chapter 4).

The same authors completed a similar study involving female students whose fathers had worked night shifts for long periods of time. They reasoned that this partial father-absence should have a similar but less profound effect than complete father-absence. All of the students included in the study had fathers engaged in manual, factory work so that socioeconomic status was relatively homogeneous throughout the sample. Quantitative scores from the ACE were significantly lower for the students whose fathers had worked the night shift than for those who had not. Again it was found that the father's "absence" when the daughter was between one and nine years of age had the most deleterious effect on the ACE scores. The authors related the absence effects in both studies to a "simple" decrease in the amount of interaction between father and child. They did not attempt a more definitive explanation of how the interaction between father and daughter influenced future ACE scores.

Several articles relating absence of the father to cognitive functioning in children have focused particularly on black families of lower socioeconomic status. Absence of a father is often one of the disadvantages these children have.

Deutsch (1960) obtained family data, observations of classroom activity and behavior, measures of academic performance, and other measures for two classes from each of the fourth, fifth, and sixth grades in a primarily black area in a "major northern city." Broken homes, which most often meant absence of the father, were the rule for 55 percent of his group. This compared with 9 percent for a comparable group of primarily white children. He indicated that broken homes were a contributing but not a primary factor in the poor school achievement of the children. The black children as a whole were about two years behind the national norms in school achievement, with those from broken homes being the farthest behind. This was particularly true for boys. Deutsch comments:

> . . . the Negro man does not have the same opportunities as the white for status mobility, job security, or individual power expression in his work relationships. These limitations inherent in the class position of the Negro man influence the Negro boy, his motivation, and his ability to operate on a delayed reward system . . . . the Negro boy very often has no close male adult with whom to identify. Further, even in an intact family, the Negro boy does not generally have the opportunity to identify with a male figure who has had a history of reinforcement for accomplishment. (p. 11)

In a similar study of 543 black and white first- and fifth-graders Deutsch and Brown (1964) looked at scores on the Lorge-Thorndike intelligence test. Among the lower-socioeconomic-status black children they found that the average IQ for those from father-present homes ran about six to eight points higher than the figure for those from father-absent homes. This held true for both boys and girls in both the first and fifth grades.

The relationship of father-absence to the child's perception of his parents

A few researchers have focused on the effect of the

father's absence on the child's perception of the absent father or perception of both parents. This effect may be of significance for the influence it may have on children's impressions of both the male sex-role and adult male authorities in general.

A study of this type that is often referred to is an older one by Bach (1946). The twenty father-absent children who were studied had fathers who had been abroad with the armed forces for from one to three years. Both they and the control group of twenty father-present children were 6 to 10 year olds, of average intelligence, and lower middle-class, urban background. He assessed the children's attitudes toward their parents by scoring their handling of a doll family during three twenty-minute play sessions. He had found in a previous study that about 75 percent of a child's productions in doll play recreate actual circumstances of the child. Bach found that the father-absent children produced an idealistic doll play pattern with the father enjoyed by and enjoying his family, receiving much affection, and showing very little exertion of authority over the family. The father-present children showed a more normal pattern in which the father played a part in punishment of children and other hostility within the family. The author commented that the father stories produced by both boys and girls from the father-absent families were like those characteristically produced by girls under father-present conditions.

One study that compared thirty second-graders, whose fathers were absent intermittently with the Navy for periods of a few days to a few months, to twenty-two comparable children of civilians did not find differences between the two groups on two tests of parental perception (Crain and Stamm, 1965).

Hetherington (1973) studied the effect of father-absence of teen-age girls' perception of men in general. The twenty-four girls who had lost their fathers through divorce tended to be more "clumsily erotic" with men, being more forward with a male interviewer, and they were more likely to have engaged in sexual intercourse than either the father-present or father-absent-through-death group. The girls who had lost their fathers through death seemed more fearful and inhibited with men, and were more delayed in their dating patterns. The girls whose parents were divorced reported more negative attitudes toward their fathers and more conflict with them. Girls from both father-absent groups were more anxious on the Taylor Manifest Anxiety Scale and believed more strongly that external factors controlled their lives. The author proposed that in both groups "the lack of opportunity for constructive interaction with a loving, attentive father has resulted in apprehension and inadequate skills in relating to males." Loss before age five was most destructive.

Qualifications

Several of the studies included in this chapter have revealed variables that seem to modulate the effects of the father's absence. Six studies indicate that the age of the child at the time of the father's absence is closely related to how much effect the absence will have on the child. Five of these indicated that sexual identification problems, personality problems, or emotional disturbances are more likely if the father's absence began in the child's first three or four years, than if the absence began later (Hetherington, 1966, 1973; Trunnell, 1968; Santrock, 1970; Biller and Bahm, 1970). One study gave a tentative indication that the father's absence during the birth to nine-year age span was related to lower college entrance exam scores than was true when the father had been absent only during the birth to four or five and older spans (Sutton-Smith, Rosenberg, and Landy, 1968). The same authors also found preliminary evidence that the father-absence effects varied depending on the sex and ordinal position of the child's siblings.

A study by Thomes (1968) is among several that suggest the effects of the father's absence may vary with the socioeconomic status of the family. The author made a comparison of 9 to 11 year old children, forty-seven from father-absent and thirty-six from father-present homes. The father-absent families were on welfare, while the control families were apparently not but were matched on such characteristics as the occupations of the fathers, occupations of the mothers, percent of mothers working outside the home, etc. On a variety of measures the author could find practically no difference between the children from the two types of families. However, the author's impressions of the fathers in the father-present homes fitted what is often described as characteristic of lower socioeconomic status fathers. They did not seem to have particularly warm or close relationships with their children. Certainly, more evidence is needed, but it may be that absence of the father may have stronger effects in middle class families where his role typically involves more interaction with his children.

Several of the authors covered in this chapter have pointed to the reaction of the mother during the father's absence as significantly influencing effects on the children (Gronseth and Tiller, 1957; Pedersen, 1966; Hoffman, 1971; Biller, 1969; Biller, 1970; Biller and Bahm, 1970; Biller, 1971). A good illustration of differences in the behavior of mothers and the related effects on the children is provided in a study sponsored by the U. S. Department of Labor (Glaser and Ross, 1970). The study was aimed at identifying significant factors in the backgrounds of seventy young black or Chicano men, some of whom were successful and some unsuccessful as judged mainly in terms of employment patterns. Both the successful and unsuccessful men had been underprivileged while growing up, and the two groups were equal on a measure of intelligence. In looking for differences in the backgrounds of the two groups of men, one thing that the authors noticed was that absence of the father in the black families was not as closely related to the success of the young man as it was in the Chicano families. The authors noted that in the Mexican-American culture the mother's role is to give unconditional love to her children, and the strong disciplinary role is reserved for the father. In contrast, either the mother or the father can exert strong control over sons in black families. Thus, in the Mexican-American family the absence of the father appeared more closely related to inadequate control over the son by the mother and a subsequent pattern of less success in society for the son.

An example of father-absence

An example of the effects of father-absence that is, fortunately, unusual rather than typical is provided in the *Report of the President's Commission on the Assassination of President John F. Kennedy* (Warren, 1964).

> Significant in shaping the character of Lee Harvey Oswald was the death of his father, a collector of insurance premiums. This occurred two months before Lee was born in New Orleans on October 18, 1939. That death strained the financial fortunes of the remainder of the Oswald family. . . . It forced Marguerite Oswald to go to work to provide for her family.

Reminding her sons that they were orphans and that the family's financial condition was poor, she placed John Pic and Robert Oswald in an orphan's home . . . until December 26, 1942, when Lee too was sent to the orphan's home. . . . (p. 377)

When Lee was about four years old Mrs. Oswald removed him and then his older brothers from the orphan's home, apparently in anticipation of her remarriage. Lee apparently became quite attached to his stepfather. Judging from several of the studies reviewed above, Lee's stepfather could have had considerable effect in filling the gap left by the father's death, but things did not work out that way. The stormy marriage of three years ended after Mrs. Oswald and her boys found her husband in another woman's apartment.

The research reviewed here indicates that the effects of the father's absence are mediated by the mother's characteristics. Here again Lee apparently was unfortunate. The commission report notes the comments of a social worker and a psychiatrist who dealt with Lee and his mother:

After her interview with Mrs. Oswald, Mrs. Siegel described her as a "smartly dressed, gray-haired woman, very self-possessed and alert and superficially affable," but essentially a "defensive, rigid, self-involved person who had real difficulty in accepting and relating to people," and who had "little understanding" of Lee's behavior and of the "protective shell he has drawn around himself." Dr. Hartogs reported that Mrs. Oswald did not understand that Lee's withdrawal was a form of "violent but silent protest against his neglect by her and represents his reaction to a complete absence of any real family life." (p. 382)

A study of the mother (Stafford, 1966) includes many

samples of her comments after the assassination that seem to exemplify her inadequate perception:

> Lee Harvey a failure? I am smiling. I find this a very intelligent boy, and I think he's coming out in history as a very fine person. . . . Killing does not necessarily mean badness. You find killing in some very fine homes for one reason or another.
>
> "I have a very unusual extrasensory perception," she had said once, "so doesn't it stand to reason that if my boy shot the President I would have *known* at the time it happened?"

After Mrs. Oswald was divorced, she worked at miscellaneous jobs. When she worked during the school year she had Lee come home to an empty house for lunch and return to it after school rather than play with other children. He apparently never gained the skills for effective social interaction, as his problems in this area are evident throughout the remainder of his life.

Mrs. Oswald and Lee moved frequently. Lee became a disciplinary problem that his mother could not control and he hit her on at least one occasion in his preteen years. When he was thirteen and they were living in New York with his brother and sister-in-law, Lee pulled out a pocket knife in an argument and threatened to use it on his sister-in-law. The Oswalds were asked to move out and this further strained the relationship between Lee and the brother, another relationship which might otherwise have helped to compensate for the father's absence.

Soon Lee was referred for a psychiatric examination because neither his mother or the school authorities were able to control his truanting from school. The personnel at the agency recommended professional help for Lee and his mother, but nothing came of the recommendation.

At sixteen Lee forged a note in his mother's name and effectively quit the school he was attending in New Orleans. He was becoming interested in communism, but, apparently as a result of the example provided by his brothers, joined the Marine Corps. His adjustment to the Marine Corps was also poor. He left the Marine Corps for Russia, but soon became as disillusioned with Russia and communism as he was with the United States and capitalism. However, he did manage to marry a Russian girl. She returned with him to the United States, and they had a child. However, the marriage was soon in difficulty. His wife later commented that he "was not a man." She asked him not to be around for his child's party a few days before Lee allegedly assassinated President Kennedy.

It is probably not possible to understand just what may have led Lee to plan an assassination. One of the clues to his reasoning was provided in the testimony of one of his Marine Corps associates:

> He looked upon the eyes of future people as some kind of tribunal, and he wanted to be on the winning side so that 10,000 years from now people would look in the history books and say, "Well, this man was ahead of his time." The eyes of the future became . . . the eyes of God. (p. 389)

Lee had attempted to formulate a better alternative to capitalism or communism which could be put into effect after both existing systems were brought down following a crisis. Perhaps the assassination was to be the crisis to bring into effect his grandiose design.

It is not possible to say either just what weight the absence of a father had in influencing Lee to be what he was. It is obvious that father-absence was an influential factor in many ways. An additional commission finding of interest was that in the year before the assassination Lee looked up some of his father's elderly relatives and visited the cemetery where his father was buried "in an effort to develop the facts of his genealogy. He obtained a large picture of his father from one of the relatives." Thus, at twenty-four years of age the father he had never seen still seemed to be of significance to Lee.

Lee Harvey Oswald was, in turn, shot by Jack Ruby, a night club manager with an eighth-grade education. Throughout his life Jack was described variously as truant, incorrigible, hot-tempered, and disobedient. Jack was described as frequently losing his temper with employees he managed and he gave numerous beatings to patrons he ejected from the clubs. Jack's father, a carpenter, was absent from the time Jack was ten and the parents separated. During the father's years in the home he had been an excessive drinker, frequently arrested on disorderly conduct and assault and battery charges.

As with Oswald, Jack Ruby's illiterate mother was incapable of filling the parental role of the inadequate and then absent father. Descriptions indicate she had an uncontrollable temper, that she lied to Jack and beat him, and was later admitted to a mental hospital on two occasions. When Jack was eleven she was unable to handle him. He was soon removed from her custody by court order and was placed in a foster home for more than a year.

Both of these cases seem to fit with much of the research in suggesting that the most destructive effects of father absence are likely to occur when a series of related factors such as the influence of the mother, siblings, socioeconomic status of the family, and others are more destructive than constructive in their effects.

Summary

Study of the effects of the father's absence on children involves the negative approach of attempting to determine what effects the father has by comparing children without fathers to those with fathers. Studies of father absence report detrimental effects on children's aggression, dependency, degree of adjustment or "psychopathology," delinquency rates, moral behavior, success in the Peace Corps or military, premarital pregnancy rates, masculinity in males, and intellectual performance.

Father-absence is, unfortunately, one of those gross variables that sounds simpler than it is. It involves a varied set of possible effects within and upon the family that is far more complicated than the simple absence of one person from the family. The effects vary, depending on the kind of relationship the father had with the children and the mother before his absence began, the cause and duration of his absence, and the availability of other adult males to the children. Father-absence effects vary also with the age of the child when the absence began, presence of other developmental problems, sex and ordinal position of any siblings, behavior of the mother during the absence, and the socioeconomic status of the family, as well as other factors.

3 fathers & sons

The influence of fathers on sons seems to be generally acknowledged by both laymen and professionals. The layman often recognizes the father's contribution to a son's characteristics as in the phrase "a chip off the old block." However, the mechanism which is responsible for the transmission of characteristics is often not apparent from the layman's observations.

The means by which behavioral characteristics are transmitted from parent to child has received considerable attention from social scientists. The means is generally referred to as the identification process, but views on the exact nature of the process are still evolving.

Sigmund Freud is usually credited with the first detailed view of the son's identification with his father, a view which is apparently still held by most psychoanalytically oriented professionals. Between about three and five years of age the son is seen as unconsciously wishing to possess his mother as a sexual partner. "Realizing" that this places him in rivalry with his father, the son becomes concerned about possible retaliation by his father. As the son becomes aware of sexual differences in anatomy he "concludes" that females have had their penis and testes removed, and that his father may do this to his son in retaliation for their rivalry over the mother. Because of this "castration anxiety" the son represses his sexual interest in his mother and identifies with the father. Freud referred to this as defensive identification. For the boy it has the effect of making him more similar to an admired father, and he expects that this similarity should decrease the possibility of the father's harming him. The identification involves the son's internalizing a conception of both parents, but particularly the father, and wishing to become like the internalized image in every respect.

A more recent view of identification is that held by social learning theorists. This view focuses on learning, particularly learning through observing and imitating the behavior of other people, rather than emphasizing the unconscious psychodynamics of Freudian theory. While a child can learn new behavior through simply observing the behavior "modeled" by another person, the likelihood of his performing the behavior is influenced by several factors. The most important factor is the reinforcement outcome for the model who exhibited the behavior. If the child sees a person punished after engaging in an act, or if there is no particular result, it is less likely that the child will imitate the behavior than if the child sees the person rewarded. For example, if a boy watches his father bring flowers to the mother and the mother praises the father for his thoughtfulness, the boy should be more likely to imitate the reinforced behavior. If instead the mother sarcastically questions the father about what he has done that he is trying to make up for, the boy should be less likely to imitate the behavior. Bandura and Walters (1965, p. 84) have pointed out that the person observing behavior modeled by another may be unable to observe any immediate consequences of the behavior, but may instead infer probable consequences based on evidence of the model's general successfulness. For this reason there has been speculation that the father of low occupational status is less frequently used as an identification model by his son than is a more successful father. Obviously, there would be many more indices of success to consider than just socioeconomic ones.

When the child does imitate the behavior of the model, the reinforcement outcome (punishment, neutral, reward) influences the probability of the child's repeating the performance. For example the boy who imitates a disliked characteristic of the father and is punished by the mother is less likely to repeat the behavior.

From this brief introduction to the social learning view of identification, it can be seen that there is not the near-exclusive identification with the same sex parent that is expected in psychoanalytic theory. Rather, the son learns behavior from various models. In a typical family it would be expected that the son would be frequently reinforced by his parents and other people for imitating the behavior of his father. In part, this would occur because behavior learned from the father would be most often appropriate to the boy's own sex, while this would not hold true for at least some of the mother's behavior. Usually the father has the advantage of being accessible as a competent male model to the boy for a greater proportion of time than is true of other models.

An alternative view of identification as it applies to the development of masculine or feminine behavior is provided by Kohlberg's (1966) cognitive-developmental view. While the psychoanalytic and social learning theories see the child as first focusing on the same sex parent, either on a psychodynamic or a reward probability basis, and then acquiring behavior appropriate to the sex of the child, the cognitive-developmental theory places the identification with the same sex parent at a much later stage in the process of sex role learning. In this approach the child is seen as first recognizing his own gender identity, and then, in the years four through eight, developing basic stereotypes of male and female sex roles. After becoming cognizant of and attracted toward the role for his sex, the child begins to identify with people of the same sex, particularly the same sex parent. The emotional attachment to the parent develops after the identification process has begun.

The concept of identification is an extremely important one for many behavioral scientists, because it is one means of accounting for the acquisition of a wide range of personality characteristics and social behaviors in children. For our purposes, we can look at a number of the efforts that have been made to examine the role of identification in the father's influence on his son, and then relate this to the identification theories.

Junior and senior high school boys and their parents were asked to answer a series of questions (Payne and Mussen, 1956). The number of identical responses given by the boy and his father, minus the number of such responses for the boy and his mother, was used as a measure of identification with the father. Scoring of stories completed by the boys and ratings of the boys by their teachers were used for measuring characteristics of the boys. Boys who were highly identified with the father were more masculine in their attitudes, and were more calm and friendly than their less highly identified peers. The boys who were more highly identified with their fathers apparently had fathers who were rewarding and affectionate toward the boys. The latter finding was

supported in a study based on interviews with mothers of
kindergarten boys (Mussen and Distler, 1960), which also
found tentative evidence that more masculine boys had
fathers who were more involved in the caretaking activities and child-rearing policies for the son.

Heilbrun (1965) studied the link between the
development of instrumental (sex appropriate) characteristics in males and the appropriateness of the sex orientation of the role model parent. Identification was determined from the similarity between university students'
descriptions of themselves on fifteen personality dimensions and their descriptions of whether the same dimensions were more characteristic of their mothers or fathers.
The students were also asked to describe themselves on a
list of 300 behavioral adjectives. Male students describing
themselves as most similar to an instrumental father
differed from females identified with an instrumental
father in 35 of the adjectives used in self-descriptions, and
18 of the 20 adjectives describing the males were sex
appropriate. Both the number of adjectives different
between the sexes and the number of sex appropriate
items used in self-description by the young men were
fewer if they were identified with expressive (sex appropriate) mothers, expressive fathers, or instrumental mothers. The author noted, as have others mentioned later in
this chapter, that identification with the opposite-sexed
parent appeared more disadvantageous for the male child
than for the female. Males identified with an expressive
mother included in their self-descriptions such unmascu-
line terms as appreciative, dependent, excitable, meek,
shy, and timid.

The desirability of the apparent link between
identification with the father and higher masculinity
scores for males may be somewhat questionable at pres-

ent as some observers of our culture find fault with the
traditional views of sex roles. A past survey of the
socialization of sex differences in 110 cultures led to
conclusions that seem even more applicable to our
culture now (Barry, Bacon, & Child, 1957). The investigators noted that smaller differences between the sexes
are associated with our "mechanized economy" which
has relatively little need for the superior average strength
of the male, and that smaller sex differences are associated with the more isolated, nuclear family in which
husband and wife must take over parts of each other's
roles at times, as they cannot call upon help from the
other adult members which would be available in an
extended family. Others (Knox and Kupferer, 1971) have
also noted that our society's emphasis on socializing the
male to themes of power, aggression, independence, and
achievement results in his later roles as husband and
father having gaps in the "behavioral and cognitive
repertoire; infant feeding, diapers, dishes, the laundro-
mat, shopping, and cooking may well confront him with
bewildering requirements for which he has no ready and
easy solutions."

However, findings in the past have been like those of
Mussen (1961) that highly masculine boys were higher in
overall adjustment, more carefree, contented, relaxed,
exuberant, happier, calmer, and smoother in social
functioning, while boys with more feminine interests
were more restless, tense, and dependent. These results
were obtained from a variety of measures of thirty-nine
subjects in the University of California Adolescent
Growth Study.

Although they were not labeled as studies of
identification, two articles found high similarity between
male high school students and their fathers to be related

to higher self-acceptance (Suinn, 1961) and acceptance by other boys (Helper, 1955).

One study of identification in 176 male university students obtained data from them on the patterning of affection and of dominance in their parents (Moulton, Liberty, Burnstein, and Altucher, 1966). The authors point out that past efforts to check independent sources about similar parent characteristics have shown that data from other sources agree fairly closely with reports by the children. Information on the pattern of guilt responses and on sex typing in the students was related to the characteristics attributed to their parents. Higher affection in the dominant parent was associated with higher levels of guilt response in the son. The son's sex typing corresponded to the sex of the dominant disciplinarian, particularly if that parent was also high in affection. The authors suggested the general principle that any "system of socialization which is arranged so that the child becomes dependent on a continued flow of affection and in which a continued supply of affection is contingent on conformity to demands is likely to produce strong internalization." "Internalization" here is probably synonymous with identification and refers to the child's adoption of the adult's characteristics. The authors note that well socialized children tend to come from homes in which the demands made on the child by both parents are consistent, and that the opposite characterizes the families of antisocial delinquents.

Analysis of parental characteristics influencing degree of parent-child similarity or degree of imitation of the parent by the child has been attempted in two studies (Hetherington, 1965; Hetherington and Frankie, 1967). The parental characteristics examined were parental dominance, warmth-hostility, and conflict, with each of these rated as the set of parents tried to resolve differences in their views on how to handle children's problems. Children from four to eleven and their parents were studied in the home situation. It was found that children were more similar to the dominant parent, and imitated that parent more. However, mother dominance was related to lower masculinity and higher imitation of the mother in boys, while father dominance did not result in such disruptively large effects upon the daughters. When fathers were dominant, boys imitated the father more while girls continued to imitate the mother. It was also found that the parent showing more warmth was more likely to be imitated, and that the dominant parent was more likely to be imitated where high conflict between the parents was noted. These findings are consistent with many of the studies of psychological disorders in males which indicate that a dominant, seemingly warm mother who is close to the son and relatively distant from the more passive father, provides a difficult setting for the son's development.

Using similar procedures to assess parental dominance, along with a measure of parental dominance based on the child's answers expressed in an interview, Biller (1969) studied the relationship between father dominance and development of sex role orientation, preference, and adoption (see Chapter 2) in kindergarten boys. Father dominance by either measure was moderately related to sex-role development with some indication that sex-role orientation may be most influenced, and that preference and adoption, which may represent subsequent stages of sex-role development, are less influenced. From some of the individual cases the author noted indications that the dominant father who encouraged similar characteristics in his son facilitated sex-role development, but the dominant father who appeared to be controlling and restrictive of his son's behavior had a less masculine son. Biller speculated that the dominant father "seems to make himself more discriminable from the mother, along with increasing the incentive value of the masculine role."

The studies of the influence of dominance on imitative behavior are consistent with laboratory research indicating the influence of a model's power on the probability of behavior being imitated by children (Bandura, Ross, & Ross, 1963; Mischel & Liebert, 1967).

Identification of the son with the father has also been found to be diminished in homes where there is marital conflict. Here the mother may be less encouraging of the son's emulation of the father (Baxter, Horton, and Wiley, 1964).

Even a more extensive review of the identification literature would probably not make possible a clear acceptance of one theory of identification and a rejection of the alternatives, partly because the theories overlap. However, from our review of several father-son identification studies it is possible to point to several considerations. The close correspondence between parental characteristics such as dominance and sex-role development in the boy is not clearly anticipated in the more general cognitive-developmental theory. Both its relative simplicity and its ability to predict child-parent imitation and the imitation of a relative stranger by the child favor social learning theory over the psychoanalytic view.

Whatever the view that is favored, mental health professionals are convinced of the importance of the identification process by their cases. Forrest (1967) describes an example from one of her psychotherapy patients that also fits rather well with the research reviewed above.

The patient was a thirty-four-year-old married man with numerous abdominal complaints and an eight-year history of barbiturate addiction. As a child he had shared his mother's contempt for a father who was subservient to the mother and her family. The patient saw his father as "inept, sloppy, and cowardly." He saw his mother as the backbone of the family, and he felt that he was the "'apple of mother's eye' because of his 'wonderful personality and good humor.'" The mother and son shared an interest in their frequent physical ailments which they saw as evidence of superior sensitivity.

His adult life was apparently a pattern of poor input and poor outcome in his educational, occupational, and marital efforts. "He feels toward himself the scorn and contempt he feels toward his father, and for the same reasons his inability to be an effective man and function in an aggressive masculine role, his need and fear of women for which he compromises himself."

Forrest uses the case to illustrate her views as to the effects the normal father has in enabling the child to see a model of someone distinct from the mother and effectively functioning in the impersonal world outside of the family.

The father's influence and maladjustment in boys

Information on the father's influence on his son's development seems to come from efforts to understand maladjustment as often as it comes from a more positive focus. Studies of homosexuality in males are of interest because they provide opportunity to compare results with studies of normal sex-role development in males.

Brown (1958) distinguished between homosexuality, as the desire for sexual activity with a person of the same sex, and "inversion," which involves identification with the psychological identity of the opposite sex. He noted that there are apparently more male than female inverts, and hypothesized that this results from the more complex identification process for males. In agreement with a number of other theorists he speculates that children of both sexes typically first identify with the mother. While the daughter can continue this appropriate identification, the son must shift to an appropriate sex-role model in his first few years of life. Absence or inadequacy of the father is seen as increasing the risk that the son will not make the shift in identification to the father and inversion, along with probable homosexual activity, would be the result.

A British study (Bene, 1965) compared eighty-three homosexual men with eighty-four married men in their responses to questions about their parents. The two groups had been matched on several variables to minimize possible background differences other than sexual orientation. It was found that the homosexual men differed from the heterosexual men on thirty-four questions concerning their relationship with their father, and on only eleven questions concerning their relationship with their mother. The results pointed much more toward the father as a person difficult to identify with than to the mother as dominant, warm, or otherwise easy to identify with. The homosexual men described far more hostility and far less affection in their past relationships with their fathers than was true for the heterosexual men. Far more of the homosexual men felt that their fathers "had no time for them, had not loved them, and had made them unhappy." Questions dealing more with the general competence of the parents also revealed significant differences in the fathers of the two groups of men. The homosexuals were more likely to indicate that their fathers "did not have a strong enough personality," "could not stand up well enough to other people," and "should have played a more important part in bringing up the children." They were less likely to describe their father as the parent who "could be firm with the children if necessary" or "made the most important decisions." The author notes that there were few indications in their results of the domineering mother that some investigators would have expected, but she notes that "if a man is weak, his wife does not have to be especially domineering to be dominant."

A number of studies are consistent with Bene's in finding a history of inadequate or absent fathers to be much more prevalent in the case of homosexual males (West, 1959; Westwood, 1960; O'Connor, 1964; Apperson & McAdoo, 1968; Evans, 1969; Hooker, 1969). The studies have varied in showing a common pattern for the mothers of male homosexuals, with the mother's contribution more evident in some of the studies of homosexuals who were patients and thus may have had other psychological disturbances as well. A number of the studies point to less adequate parental behavior in both the father and the mother as being much more frequent in the childhood of male homosexuals.

One study of homosexual behavior in male juvenile delinquents (Greenstein, 1966) did not obtain findings like the rest, perhaps because of the types of measures employed in the research, but it did point to instances of a few fathers who were so physically close with their sons that it may have encouraged the development of homosexual activity.

Bieber and his associates (1962) found results similar to most previous studies in their comparisons of 106 homosexual men and 100 heterosexual men, both of which groups were also in treatment by psychoanalysts. Each therapist filled out a twenty-six-page questionnaire on his patients. Key findings pointed to a close-binding, intimate mother who was dominant and minimizing toward a husband who was a detached and hostile father in the history of the homosexuals. They regarded none of the fathers of the homosexuals as being reasonably normal parents. The authors speculated that the son may react to the father's detachment by seeking to fill his yearning for an adequate relationship with the father by turning to other males. The authors noted also that some of the fathers of homosexuals had punished masculine behavior in the son, perhaps because it was viewed by the father as competing with him. The authors provide a number of case reports. Some of the characteristics of the family in one of the cases are representative of the detached hostile fathers.

The son in this case recalled a parental quarrel when he was about four, which resulted in his mother's announcing that she alone would raise him. The father had a separate room and was like a boarder in the house. The father was quite fastidious and protective of his possessions. He wouldn't kiss either the mother or the son on the lips, and avoided using glasses they had drunk from. Even when the patient was in high school he was not allowed to use his father's typewriter. When the patient was three and a half he was given a tricycle that was too tall for him. His feet did not reach the pedals.

"I got on to ride it, but I started to roll down the hill. My father was standing there—tall, still, dressed very correctly. He watched but did nothing to try to stop the tricycle. I was terrified. I went racing down the hill and fell off. My father just continued to stand there." (p. 194)

The patient felt that his father's prudishness was related to the idea that the son developed of sex as "filthy and revolting." Support of the son's assertiveness or time spent with the boy was missing. When the son finished high school the father advised him to take a job in another country, but the son saw this advice as an effort to get rid of him and refused to go. The son developed feelings of both fear and hatred toward the father.

Westwood (1960) points out that there are at least twenty-two theories on the causes of homosexuality, ranging from regarding it as a hereditary defect to attributing it to lack of sexual success with the opposite sex. Among other findings his study yielded interesting comments of homosexuals on the sex education they had received (p. 22).

Mother once asked if I knew about things and I said I did, but I didn't.

Father said he would explain everything when I was seventeen. By then he realized it was too late.

When I was fourteen my father flung a sex book at me and told me to read it and then quickly left the room. He was quite embarrassed. . . . I scanned through it but I wasn't interested and didn't really take it in.

My father made one blundering effort. He handed me a book and mumbled something about me finding this useful. I read it but we never discussed the subject.

Only 13 percent of the homosexuals could remember

attempts by either of their parents to give them sex instruction, but this may not be much different from the experience of heterosexuals. Attitudes toward sex that the parents communicate indirectly may be more significant.

While many of the twenty-two theories Westwood refers to have little support or have been discredited, it remains true that it is far from possible to attribute all cases of homosexuality to the same cause. In Westwood's study, for example, 25 to 30 percent of the homosexual men described their childhood as happy, secure, and unemotional, with both parents average or better in their apparent marital happiness. They had good relationships with their fathers, and their mothers were not possessive. The influence of the father may well be the greatest factor in the development of homosexuality in males, but it is neither a necessary nor a sufficient explanation of male homosexuality.

Some readers may be surprised to see homosexuality listed here as a type of maladjustment. The current emphasis on "gay lib" implies in part that homosexuality is merely a sexual choice and not a problem. Perhaps that is sometimes the case, but the studies referred to here also included a great deal of information relating homosexuality to many other forms of maladjustment. Perhaps regarding homosexuality as simply an alternative pattern of sexual behavior is a misguided byproduct of the current mood of liberation and equality.

The question of sex-role behavior of the father and its influence on psychological disorders in the son is involved in a study by Kayton and Biller (1970) that has some very interesting implications. Eighty adult males participated in the study. Twenty of the subjects were categorized as normal, twenty as neurotic, twenty as paranoid schizophrenics and twenty as other schizophrenics. The men in each category were similar in age, education, intact homes, and socioeconomic status. The men were asked to indicate which of fifteen paragraphs describing particular behavioral traits characterized their fathers and which characterized their mothers. Five of the paragraphs described the traits of achievement, aggression, autonomy, dominance, and endurance, all traits which describe the instrumental orientation which several investigators find to be characteristic of males in our culture. Five paragraphs describe the traits of abasement, affiliation, deference, nurturance, and succorance, which describe the expressive orientation characteristic of most females in our culture. The remaining five characteristics were non-sex-typed. The normal males chose the descriptions as characterizing their fathers significantly more than their mothers on 80 percent of the masculine traits, while this was true for only 20 or 40 percent of the masculine traits when rated by the three disturbed groups. The normal males chose the descriptions as characterizing their mothers significantly more than their fathers on 60 percent of the feminine traits, while this was true on 20 percent of the feminine traits rated by neurotics, and on none of the feminine traits as rated by the schizophrenic groups. The results were consistent with previous studies using more direct measures of parental characteristics in pointing to the frequency of inappropriate parental sex-roles in the history of those with psychological disorders. The authors point to the helpfulness of distinctive sex-roles in the parents for providing "clearly discriminable sex-role boundaries which can facilitate the child's identification."

These results have implications for one type of change that may be occurring in our society. It is illustrated in answers that the author has seen to questions asked in parent interviews conducted by several hundred students as part of their classwork. Two of the questions asked of parents of widely different ages, occupations, national origins, etc., are "Do you think that raising boys or raising girls are very different tasks for a parent?" and "Do you believe there are usually differences between the child-rearing approach of mothers and the child-rearing approach of fathers?" While most of the answers are along fairly traditional lines, a few liberal young couples seem to echo the "unisex" theme in society by indicating that they are raising their children to "buck that classic male and female role," in some cases specifying that they are raising their children identically regardless of their biological sex. Results like those above suggest the possibility that unisex applied to child rearing may have far more complex ramifications than just being an "advance" in social liberation. Perhaps these well-meaning young parents have not detected the distinction between equal opportunity for both sexes and both sexes becoming identical.

It is possible to compare Kayton and Biller's findings concerning parental sex-role and psychological disorders in males with those obtained in a study (Rabkin, 1964) which was similar in comparing the parents of 114 ten-year-old boys who were diagnosed as schizophrenic or neurotic, had behavior disorders, or were normal. There was again evidence of sex-role problems in the parents and identification problems for the boys in the disturbed categories. The schizophrenic boys described their mothers as the stronger and smarter parent, boss of the family, and the parent they wanted to grow up to be like more often than was the case for the normal boys. The fathers of the schizophrenic boys were described by them more often as nurturant, a characteristic normally expected to be more true of the mother. The neurotic boys described their fathers as the boss of the house, and as punitive, and they more often wanted to grow up like the mother than was true for normal boys. The boys with behavior disorders differed from the normals in their frequency of describing the father as more punitive and frightening, and the mother as more competent and the parent they would prefer to grow up like. The results seem to support those of Kayton and Biller in pointing to the diminution or reversal of parental sex-roles in the parents of males with psychological disorders. A reservation about both studies is that parental descriptions by individuals with psychological disorders may be less accurate than that of normals. However, in studying adult male and female schizophrenics, McClelland and Watt (1968) describe sex-role effects that are not merely confused responses but distinct behavior patterns. They suggest that *alienation* from one's primary sex-role is part of the history of many schizophrenics. For some behaviors the alienation from one's own sex-role involves adapting with behavior of the opposite sex because it is the only alternative.

One unique study looks at the father's influence on serious psychological disorders in forty-two French and English male poets (Martindale, 1972). The author studied biographical information on poets who became eminent during a time span of about two-hundred years. It was found that in 81 percent of the poets for whom biographical information cites such disorders as alcoholism, "breakdowns," suicide, or commitment to an asylum, the fathers were either absent or there was mention of the poet's friction with the father and over-closeness to females, feminine behaviors in the poet, or a weak and passive father. The author appropriately notes the tentativeness of data gathered in this method.

Additional support for the influence of many of these aspects of the father's behavior upon personality-social development in boys can be found in many of the studies searching for the causes of juvenile delinquency. One of the largest efforts is the longitudinal study of five-hundred delinquent males and five-hundred nondelinquents begun in 1948 when the boys averaged about fourteen and one-half years of age (Glueck & Glueck, 1968). The boys in both groups lived in underprivileged areas in Boston when the study began and are matched in age, ethnic origin, and global intelligence. Conditions detrimental to adequate development of the child appear to be almost overwhelming in both groups, with many of the conditions being present in an even higher proportion of the delinquents' homes than is true for the nondelinquents. Both parents of the delinquents were more likely to have come from families characterized by severe psychological disorders, were more likely to have married because the female was pregnant, and were more likely themselves to have psychological disorders, physical illnesses, histories of delinquent behavior, and intellectual retardation than was the case for the parents of nondelinquents. More of the delinquents' homes had been broken by separation, divorce, death, or prolonged absence of either parent, but particularly the father. Where the fathers were present 40 percent of them were described as showing warmth, sympathy, and consistent affection toward the boys, as compared to a rate of 80 percent for the fathers of the nondelinquent boys. Overly strict and/or inconsistent disciplinary practices were more than twice as prevalent among fathers of delinquents as they were among fathers of nondelinquents. Mothers of the delinquents were described as "cripplingly overprotective" or permissive much more frequently than was the case for mothers of nondelinquents.

The findings point to multiple factors influencing delinquency with many of them related to the fathers of these boys who later "ripened into adult criminals."

Andry (1960, 1962) also found early adolescent delinquent boys to feel more unloved by their fathers than was true for nondelinquents, to prefer to deal with the mother when in trouble, and to be more fearful of the father than of the mother. While the nondelinquents and delinquents were similar in recognizing the father as the head of the household, the delinquents were less likely to obey him. Some indications of problems for the delinquent boys in identifying with their fathers were present in their frequent answer that they had their mothers' "ways," while the nondelinquents indicated that they had both parents' or their fathers' "ways." The author also found that the fathers of delinquents had less leisure time with their sons and were less involved with them in hobbies and outings. When the parents were questioned, the author was surprised to find the parents confirming the aspects of inadequate fathering indicated by their delinquent sons. Although the parents were frequently aware of the problems they were ineffective in doing much to solve them. The author's conclusions were based on a sample of eighty delinquents and eighty similar nondelinquents in England.

It may be fitting to close the discussion of the undesirable effects of fathers on sons with an example from the most undesirable son in this century.

Adolf Hitler's father, Alois Hitler, had several marriages or quasimarital relationships (Heiden, 1944; Bullock, 1964). When he was forty-eight he married for the third time. His new wife was twenty-five and he had raised her for years as a foster-daughter. She was actually either a second cousin or a niece to Alois, with the exact relationship unclear because of past irregularities in relationships within the family, and Alois himself was considered illegitimate.

The marriage resulted in five children but three died within a few years after birth. Adolf Hitler was one of the two who survived. Also in the home were a half-brother and a half-sister to Adolf. Their mother had been a hotel cook with whom Alois had lived prior to the death of his first wife.

Alois worked for the Austrian government as a rifle-carrying border guard, but retired when Adolf was small. Alois was a short-tempered, prematurely inactive, old man. Adolf was apparently beaten by his father, perhaps sometimes over their disagreement about Adolf's wish to become a painter. While he met with sternness in contacts with his father, Adolf was apparently quite able to exploit his weak mother. Teachers, fellow pupils, and neighbors described Adolf as a "roughneck, an eloquent, loud-voiced ringleader in children's games, planning a trip around the world with his comrades, bringing knives and axes to school with him." His father died when Adolf was thirteen.

> Adolf Hitler hated his father, and not only in his subconscious; by his insidious rebelliousness he may have brought him to his grave a few years before his time; he loved his mother deeply, and himself said that he had been a "mother's darling." Constantly humiliated and corrected by his father, . . . he seems to have grown accustomed to the idea that right is always on the side of the stronger. . . . (p. 50)

The pattern of one weak, permissive, affectionate parent and one harsh, rejecting parent is a destructive one involving great inconsistency in the handling of the child. If the father had been stern but accepting, Adolf

Hitler's characteristics and the course of history might have been much different. As it was, Adolf may have had an ambivalent identification with his father, imitating some of the authoritarian characteristics which enabled the father to dominate his weaker wife and family, but also rejecting aspects of the hated father. Adolf's identification with the sexual aspect of the male role has often been questioned. His involvement with the opposite sex came late and his relationship with his "mistress" has still not become clear.

The father's influence on
intellectual ability and occupational choice

Some information is available that shows paternal influence on the effectiveness or patterning of cognitive ability in males. The connection between the discipline patterns of parents and the presence of cognitive disturbances in college age males was studied by Heilbrun & Orr, 1966. The students were asked to sort ninety-six cards varying in three different dimensions into four compartments. The students who described a rejecting (highly controlling-low nurturant) pattern of behavior for their fathers performed more poorly at the conceptual task than students who described an accepting pattern (low controlling-highly nurturant). Those describing patterns of low control-low nurturant or high control-high nurturant behavior in the father performed at an intermediate level on this task. The authors found the same effects to be linked to the mother's behavior patterns toward the son. They reasoned that the rejecting treatment by parents leads to low self-esteem, and, as a result, less effective cognitive performance.

The greater interest of boys in objects and in more objective tasks as contrasted with the interest of girls in people has been linked to the greater interest and intensity of fathers in their differentiation of behavior regarded as appropriate for boys and girls (Goodenough, 1957). The differences were found in the drawings and verbalizations of children from age two through the preschool ages. This of course relates closely to the instrumental vs. expressive difference in the sexes and the father's influence upon it (see Chapter 4). The special interest of the father in orienting his son toward objective accomplishment in the world outside the family is emphasized in a study showing that fathers of mentally retarded sons show more extreme reactions to that situation than do the fathers of daughters (Tallman, 1965).

The vocational adjustment of males as it is influenced by their fathers is the focus of a study which involved interviewing 142 males when they were ninth-graders and again when they were seven years beyond high school (Bell, 1969). The researchers made note of points in the transcribed interviews where the subjects referred to the positive or negative examples of other people around them and how these examples influenced their educational, vocational, and related behaviors. At the ninth-grade level the subjects referred more often to their fathers as role models than they did to other models mentioned. Most of the references were to the father as a positive example; and the boys whose fathers were most positive occupational role models in grade nine were most likely to have attained their occupational goals ten years later and were higher in occupational satisfaction. The findings for the men when they were seven years out of high school indicated that by then the father's influence had diminished in favor of other adult relatives, peers, teachers, and employers.

In studying the parental identification and vocational interests of university undergraduates, Crites (1962) found that two hundred males who came to the vocational-educational service of the campus counseling center were weaker in identification with their fathers than were other male students. He found also that only identification with the father correlated with the students' interest patterns on the Strong Vocational Interest Blank. Those strongly identified with the father tended to be interested in business detail occupations, while those with a less strong father identification showed a varied pattern of interests.

Further evidence of the father's influence on his son's career choice comes from a study of 76,015 males entering 246 colleges and universities (Werts, 1961). The young men "overchose" the same occupations as their father, or a similar one, in each occupation studied by Werts. For example, 35 to 45 percent of the sons of medical men chose medical careers (physician, dentist, pharmacist, veterinarian) as compared to 10 to 15 percent of the sons of men connected with the physical or social sciences. The author speculated that fathers in the physical sciences may encourage an interest in the "why and how of things" while those in the social sciences may encourage an interest in people. Of course the correspondence between the father's occupation in the physical or social sciences and the son's tendency to choose a like occupation could also be attributed to observational learning ("identification") on the part of the son as well as direct encouragement.

An illustration that is probably a good example, but at the same time an exception in many ways, is the life of British Prime Minister Winston Churchill (Carter, 1965). He pursued a career in Parliament as his father Lord Randolph Churchill had. Yet it was not a simple case of

close identification of the son with the father. Winston
was treated in a manner common for that time, with a
nannie, Mrs. Everest, caring for him in the nursery
portion of the house. Parents were remote people "pro-
tected from noise, intrusion, worry, interruption—in fact
from children, in whom all such hazards are inherent."
At seven Winston was dispatched to a private school, and
he later attended Sandhurst.

While both of Winston's parents remained at a
considerable distance physically and emotionally, their
influence upon him, particularly that of the father, was
still great.

> But while Mrs. Everest held his heart and his mother
> shone for him in evening skies, it was the image of his
> father which dominated and obsessed his being. It was
> in truth an image of his own creation that he wor-
> shipped. He did not know his father, nor does Lord
> Randolph appear to have made any attempt to know
> his son, whose intelligence he rated so low that he
> considered him unfit to practice at the bar. He con-
> signed him to the army after a brief glance at a game of
> soldiers Winston was playing with his brother on the
> nursery floor. (p. 27)

Though there seems to have been little positive
thought of the father for his son, the son consistently
held his father as the hero to imitate. Perhaps the nannie
played a part in encouraging this emulation, in the way
that might in other circumstances be practiced by the
mother. Lord Randolph died when Winston was twenty-
two, and at a time when Winston felt he and his father
were beginning to become close.

> The greatest and most powerful influence in my
> early life was of course my father. Although I had
> talked with him so seldom and never for a moment on
> equal terms, I conceived an intense admiration and

affection for him; and after his early death, for his memory. I read industriously almost every word he had ever spoken and learnt by heart large portions of his speeches. I took my politics almost unquestioningly from him. . . . He seemed to own the key to everything or almost everything worth having. (pp. 27-28)

Summary

The father's influence on the son seems to be an influence that has been more easily understood and appreciated by both laymen and theorists than have other aspects of the father's influence. An important process involved is that of identification or observational learning. Where the father is interested in and involved with the son, both generally accepting him and appropriately monitoring his behavior, and where the father provides a successful model of behaviors for his son, the son generally will acquire many of the characteristics of the father and initially use his father's example as a general guide to his own career. To become like the father who is reasonably admirable and desirable is regularly associated with appropriate masculinity, popularity, and general good adjustment for the boy.

If the father fails in any of these aspects, the risks of the son's incurring such problems as homosexuality, psychological disorders, or a delinquent pattern are increased, although there remain many ways in which adequate adjustment for the boy can be achieved.

4 fathers &
daughters

Research relating the development of boys to the influences of their fathers, as well as their mothers, has received considerable attention. The relationship between mothers and daughters has also received fairly extensive consideration. The role of the father in the development of his daughter seems to have received the least attention.

The inattention to the father-daughter relationship seems surprising in view of the emphasis on that relationship in psychoanalytic theories. The esoteric view of the psychoanalytic theorists on the father's part in the daughter's development is well summarized in Hall and Lindzey's review of Freud:

> In the first place, she exchanges her original love object, the mother, for a new object, the father. Why this takes place depends upon the girl's reaction of disappointment when she discovers that a boy possesses a protruding sex organ, the penis, while she has only a cavity. Several important consequences follow from this traumatic discovery. In the first place, she holds her mother responsible for her castrated condition which weakens the cathexis for the mother. In the second place, she transfers her love to the father be-

79

cause he has the valued organ which she aspires to share with him. However, her love for the father and for other men as well is mixed with a feeling of envy because they possess something she lacks. Penis envy is the female counterpart of castration anxiety in the boy, and collectively they are called the *castration complex*. She imagines that she has lost something valuable, while the boy is afraid he is going to lose it. To some extent, the lack of a penis is compensated for when a woman has a baby, especially if it is a boy baby. (1957, p. 54)

Tess Forrest (1966) provides a neoanalytic view of the father's role in the daughter's development, a view that reflects some of the recent research on this topic. She describes the father's masculinity as significant in supporting the mother and in relating the family to the outside world. She suggests that the father's influence on the daughter begins earlier than has been appreciated by other psychoanalytic theorists.

She must learn paternal trust during infancy when she learns maternal trust. Especially from her father does the infant girl need confirmation of her desirability as a female and affirmation of her value as a different and separate person. His gentle tenderness communicates to her his pleasure in her femininity. Father, by comparison with mother, has a sharper eye, a firmer grip, a rougher cheek, a deeper voice. He is nonetheless equally tender, loving, warm, and safe, and the infant girl can feel herself lovingly cradled by a man's arms and comforted by a man's voice. Contact with the father opens the door of the mother-infant dyad to the possibility and pleasure of triadic union and secondary dependency. (pp. 20-30)

The author suggests that the daughter's experiences with the father from early infancy are related to the daughter's later ability to trust other males, and the ease

with which the father and the daughter can accept her
fuller sexual development in adolescence. The father's
influence on the daughter is described as partly mediated
through the daughter's identification with the mother. If
an optimal marital relationship exists between the parents, the daughter is influenced vicariously by the characteristics the spouses exhibit in marital interaction. "Her
identification with her mother renders the daughter
sensitive to the nuances of father's feelings, attitudes, and
opinions of women. She naturally considers these a
reflection on her and a direction for her." (p. 32)

Beginning with the mid-1960s a series of significant
theoretical and research efforts have related numerous
aspects of the daughter's development to the father's
influence. Most of these authors have departed from the
psychoanalytic view of the girl's development. One of the
most significant articles was written by Miriam Johnson
(1963). She noted that in the existing research on identification between children and parents, many of the findings were contradictory to existing theory, and she
offered a theoretical proposal that would better integrate
these findings.

Johnson begins with a modified definition of
identification, "as the internalization, not of a total
personality or of personality traits, but of a reciprocal
role relationship that is functional at a particular period
in the child's development." She assumes that the child's
initial identification is with the mother, but that it is a
later identification with the father which is crucial for
sex-role learning in both males and females. The differences in the behavior of the two parents are related to
differences in their own sex roles. Drawing on the work
of sociologist Talcott Parsons, Johnson describes the
mother as typically more of an "expressive" role player, a

person concerned more about relationships among people. The father, as a male, is more of an "instrumental" role player, a person concerned with the pursuit of goals beyond the immediate interpersonal situation.

The mother is inclined to respond to both sons and daughters primarily as children. Johnson does not describe the mother's nurturant and supportive response to her children as preventing her from valuing and encouraging sex-appropriate behavior on the children's part. She does emphasize that it is the father's differentiated response to his sons and daughters, and his stronger concern about the development of their sex-appropriate behavior that has the greatest impact on children's sex role learning. In terms of their roles while interacting with the children, the mother is described as expressive with children of either sex, while the father is described as expressive with his daughters and instrumental with his sons. At a less abstract level the father is described as more appreciative, less demanding with his daughter and responsive to her attractiveness, while with the son he is more demanding and more of a mentor. In each case the father's reaction is representative of the sex role demands that the world outside the family will make upon the children.

One of the studies showing the greater concern of the father about differentiated sex role development in children was conducted by Goodenough (1957). In children only two to four years of age it was found that girls focused more on people in their verbalizations, and when drawing, 45 percent of the girls drew people as compared to 11 percent of the boys. Interviews with the parents indicated that both parents expected boys and girls to differ in their interest in persons, but it was particularly the fathers who showed the greatest interest and intensity in their differentiation of boys' and girls' behavior.

Johnson refers to a number of empirical studies which yielded results that were generally unanticipated by their authors, but can be encompassed by her theory. The studies that she refers to indicate that the father's reaction to boys and girls is more differentiated than is the reaction of the mother. The main areas of behavior involved are discipline and sex role learning. She also refers to a number of the identification studies which have not found the expected relationship—that of sons being more similar to their fathers than their mothers, and daughters being more similar to their mothers than their fathers. These studies have typically involved having males and females fill out some measure of personal characteristics, both to describe themselves and then separately to describe each of their parents. The relationship between similarity of the parent and child of the same sex and the child's standing on some measure of adjustment is often studied. While similarity between father and son is related to better adjustment of the son, some of the studies cited by Johnson indicate an association between father-daughter similarity and better adjustment for the daughter. She finds clearest support in the study by Sopchak (1952), who had 108 college students fill out the Minnesota Multiphasic Personality Inventory (MMPI) four different times at one-week intervals. On one occasion they were to fill it out for themselves, and on three other occasions they were to complete it as their father, mother, and "most people" would. The identification score was the number of answers that were identical between the person's self responses and the responses given on the other three tests. For both men and women the greatest mean similarity was between their own test and that for the parent of the same sex. The surprising finding for the female students was that tendencies toward abnormality on the masculinity, psychasthenia, and schizophrenia scales of the MMPI were correlated significantly but inversely with identification with the father. The result for the masculinity scale was particularly interesting since it indicated that more feminine women were more closely identified with their fathers than were masculine women.

Subsequent investigators have described similar but not completely identical findings. Heilbrun (1968) begins with the assumption that "a child can model after both parents to varying degrees, so that identification-mediated behavior of the child may include the attributes of both parents." He notes along with Johnson that boys' identification with fathers has consistently been found to relate to good adjustment, while the comparable effect of girl-mother identification has rarely been found. There are numerous indications that the male role has been more highly regarded in our culture, and that masculine behaviors in females are better tolerated than are feminine behaviors in males. Heilbrun and Fromme (1965) suggested that the aspect of identification that is most significant for the person's adjustment is the extent to which the person acquires behavior from parental identification which is compatible with the stereotypical values of her or his social group.

The authors include the relative masculinity-femininity of both parents in their study of the relationship between parental identification and adjustment in 523 university undergraduates. The measure of identification used included sex-typed items so that the masculinity-femininity of either parent could be determined from the student's parent descriptions. The index of adjustment used was the student's use of the university's counseling services, with nonuse indicating good adjustment. Adjusted males tended to identify with masculine fathers while more seriously maladjusted males tended to identify with less masculine fathers. In females, adjustment corresponded with identification with a mother low in femininity, while more maladjusted females identified with highly feminine mothers. Heilbrun (1968) indicates that the girls who tended to identify with masculine fathers were better adjusted than those who identified with feminine mothers. Since these results are drawn from work with college students, it could be argued that the girls with the more feminine identification pattern were more prone to problems in the competitive college situation, and perhaps would not have similar problems in noncompetitive situations. The author argues against this interpretation, since in his experience the types of problems that female college students bring to a college counseling center are seldom centered around academic competition and achievement.

Heilbrun notes that Johnson used the term "identification" in an unusual way in her discussion of the father's influence on the child's sex role learning. She used it to refer to the father's differential response to his sons and daughters. Heilbrun reasons that the same results could follow from the more typical concept of identification, that in which the child acquires behavior by imitating behavior of the model. He notes Johnson's evidence that the father plays both an instrumental and an expressive role. He reasons that this enables the son to learn masculine behavior in his interaction with the father, while the daughter could learn some part of her feminine behavior from the more feminine model the father exhibits in his interaction with her. In addition, the daughter could learn some of the father's instrumental behavior from him, which would facilitate the girl's adjustment in some situations. In this series of related studies, Heilbrun has obtained several findings in support of his interpretation: (1) masculine fathers are more nurturant toward their daughters than toward their sons; (2) male and female college students identified with masculine fathers had most extensive and appropriate sex role behaviors; (3) more masculine girls tended to be masculine-father-identified and showed a capacity for both expressive and instrumental behavior in discussion groups; and (4) more feminine girls tended to be feminine-mother-identified and limited to expressive behavior. His reference to masculine and feminine girls may be confusing. He is referring to those who were above or below the average score on the masculinity-femininity scale of an adjective check list. Thus, it may be that few, if any, of the girls' scores were extreme. The finding does seem contradictory to the study cited above by Sopchak which found father-identified girls to be more feminine. Heilbrun concludes:

> . . . most importantly, even a conservative interpretation allows that a father-identification can mediate a healthy adjustment in the adolescent girl, and must be considered as one of the "normal" developmental channels for establishing a satisfactory female sex-role identity. Any theory of sex-role development, psychoanalytic or behavioristic, that cannot gracefully embrace this apparent paradox may be in need of revision. (1968, p. 86)

In a previous study (1965) Heilbrun compared females who were identified with expressive mothers, the usually expected combination, to females who were identified with instrumental fathers. The latter group significantly more often described themselves as self-confident, while the expressive mother-identified females described themselves significantly more often as considerate, fearful, gentle, obliging, silent, submissive, and trusting. The author was comparing the person's identification with expressive or instrumental mothers or fathers to a self-description on a 300-item adjective checklist in a study of 418 university undergraduates. Heilbrun reached two conclusions from this part of the comparisons. One was that the differences cited between the two female groups were relatively few out of 300 items. Secondly, the differences found suggest that "instrumental-father identified females do not assume blatant instrumental qualities relative to very expressive females, but rather maintain an expressive orientation which lacks the passive character of extreme expressiveness."

In an article reviewing the father-daughter relationship as it affects the personality development of the female, Biller and Weiss (1970) attempt to clarify the relationship between the relative femininity of the daughter and her identification with the father. They suggest that a healthy father identification for a daughter involves understanding and empathizing with him and accepting some of his values and attitudes, rather than wanting to be masculine like him. They concur with Heilbrun in noting the evidence that the daughter may gain a wider, more adaptable range of behaviors from identification with a competent masculine father. They suggest that the daughter is unlikely to reject her femininity and imitate the father's strictly masculine behaviors unless the mother defaults in her role.

Part of the evidence that Biller and Weiss refer to is a study of a large group of female undergraduates by Wright and Tuska (1966). They asked 2650 students to rate themselves between twenty-six pairs of bipolar adjectives (semantic differential). A group of 1892 who had rated themselves "very feminine" were contrasted with 210 who had rated themselves as "slightly feminine," or as "to some extent masculine." Comparing the two groups on six basic factors composed of the remaining bipolar adjectives yielded a self-description for the "feminine" group as significantly more narcissistic, confident, and comfortable, while the "masculine" women rated themselves significantly more forceful, intelligent, and responsive. The coeds were also asked to indicate which parent was most important in nineteen different parent-child relationships (e.g., "Whom did you want to be with most?, Who did the most with you?"). The analysis indicated that the "masculine" women were more influenced by the father, had a relatively frustrating, anti-pathetic relationship with their mother, and felt less well understood in general. The "feminine" women described an admired and influential mother, and they described a more favorable image of the father in his masculine role.

The rather contradictory picture of the well adjusted female who accomplished her adjustment through acquiring some of her father's masculine characteristics is clarified some by Connell and Johnson's (1970) study of the relationship between sex-role identification (Gough's Femininity Scale) and self-esteem (Coopersmith's Self-Esteem Inventory). In studying 143 eighth-graders in a Catholic school they found boys high in masculine sex-role identification to be significantly higher in self-esteem. Self-esteem scores can apparently be taken as a fairly good index of overall adjustment (Coopersmith, 1967). For girls there was no apparent relationship between the two characteristics.

It appears, therefore, that the adolescent female may

adopt either role and receive positive reinforcement for adopting either role. She can adopt a somewhat masculine orientation and find reward value in the competence and mastery associated with the masculine stereotype. Or, she can adopt the feminine orientation and receive positive reinforcement for responding to a socially expected and maintained stereotype. Consequently, the female can apparently adopt either sex-role orientation without seriously affecting feelings of self-esteem. (p. 8 of extended report)

Further evidence of differences in the relative complexity of the development of boys and girls was found by Mussen and Rutherford (1963). They administered the IT Scale measure of masculinity-femininity of interests and a doll play situation for deriving an estimate of the parents' behavior toward fifty-seven female and forty-six male first-graders. Information was obtained from part of their parents through an interview with the mothers and through administration to mothers and fathers of a femininity scale, self-acceptance scales, and a check list of play and games encouraged by the parents. The masculinity of boys proved to be significantly related only to the warmth and nurturance of their fathers. This was in contrast to a considerably more complex pattern for the girls. The warmth and nurturance as well as the self-acceptance of mothers was related to femininity in girls. In addition, the fathers of highly feminine girls were more masculine than the fathers of the less feminine girls, and also provided more encouragement and stimulation of sex appropriate play and game activities. In fact, the fathers of highly feminine girls had almost the same score as the girls' mothers in encouraging sex differentiated activities in their daughters.

Brim's study of siblings' effects on each other points again to differences in the personality formation of boys and girls, and also helps to confirm that it is possible for girls to gain certain "masculine" characteristics without losing their feminine characteristics. Brim (1958) started from the hypothesis that "interaction between the two persons leads to assimilation of roles, to the incorporation of elements of the role of the other into the actor's role." He looked at data on five- and six-year-olds with older siblings of different ages and sexes. The children's characteristics had been rated by their teachers on fifty-eight traits, and Brim divided these traits into those that were more masculine or more feminine. The young girls who had older brothers had substantially more masculine traits than the girls who had older sisters, thus supporting the hypothesis in pointing to a masculine influence from the brother. Relevant to this discussion of the father's influence on the daughter, Brim noted, "the acquisition of male traits does not seem to reduce the number of feminine traits of the girls who have brothers. The more accurate interpretation is that acquisition of such traits adds to their behavioral repertoire, probably with a resultant dilution of their femininity in behavior but not a displacement."

Brim also found that boys with older sisters were substantially more feminine than those with older brothers. For some reason, however, the additional feminine traits of the boys with older sisters seemed to have displaced rather than supplemented masculine traits. The author noted that influences of siblings would be in addition to major influences from parents.

A check on the accuracy of parents' knowledge of their children's behavior and ability to predict to a new situation was provided in a study by Nakamura and Rogers (1969). Mothers and fathers of thirty-nine pre-school-age children were asked to rate twenty items of autonomous behavior according to how common or uncommon these were to their children. Several weeks later the children began attending nursery school for the first time, and their actual behavior was observed. It was found that mothers did better at predicting their sons' behavior than their daughters' and better than the fathers had predicted their sons' behavior. However, the fathers predicted their daughters' behavior better than their sons' and better than the mothers had predicted their daughters' behavior. The authors hesitated to speculate much about these findings based on a small sample, but they do seem to fit with a series of findings questioning the common assumption that fathers may be involved in raising their sons, but they are little involved with their daughters.

A number of studies have been conducted which focus on differences between fathers and mothers in their behavior toward sons and daughters, respectively. In a two-part study Droppleman and Schaefer (1963) first studied 165 seventh grade children in a Catholic school, and then studied 70 eleventh-grade children in a public school. Both groups showed a similar pattern of responses to a 260-question parent-behavior inventory. Both boys and girls described the mother as higher on scales involving love, nurturance, or affection, as well as on the use of covert, indirect methods of control. The cross-sexed effects occurred on scales involving irritability and nagging or extreme autonomy and lax discipline. On these scales girls described their fathers as allowing them more autonomy and lax discipline and as being less irritable or nagging. The girls described their mothers in the reverse fashion. Incidentally, the girls reported receiving significantly more love, affection, or nurturance from both parents than the boys did.

A similar pattern of cross-sexed effects resulted from an unusual experiment conducted by Rothbart and Maccoby (1966). They studied ninety-eight mothers and thirty-two fathers of children enrolled in parent-involved nursery schools. In several group meetings the parents listened to the tape-recorded voice of a four-year-old child. A child was used whose voice was not clearly identifiable as to sex. Some of the groups of parents were told they were listening to a boy, while others were told the same tape-recording was made by a girl. The parent was asked to imagine that he or she was reading at home, and that the recorded voice was his child playing in the next room with a one-year-old baby. The parents were allowed time to write down what their response would be to the child's remarks. The twelve remarks included these examples: "Daddy (or Mommy), come look at my puzzle." "Daddy, help me. I don't like this game—I'm gonna break it!" In scoring the parents' responses, they found that mothers showed more permissiveness and positive attention toward their sons, while fathers showed more permissiveness and positive attention toward their daughters. The pattern of results was unexpected by the authors. Both this study and the one immediately preceding it support the existence of a unique relationship between daughters and their fathers, an influence on the daughter that may be lacking if the father is ineffectual in his role or is absent.

The findings described so far in this chapter involve the significance of the father for the normal development of feminine, well adjusted behavior in his daughter. There are also a large number of studies indicating the father's influence on the development of various other characteristics of girls. Part of these studies involve the effects of father absence and are described in Chapter 2.

Others are primarily concerned with parental influences in the development of characteristics of children in general, and these are included in Chapter 5. There remain a smaller number of studies which have focused particularly on the father's influence on the development of his daughter's characteristics, and it seems appropriate to describe some of these here. In view of the reassessment of the father's significance which is evident in the work of the authors reviewed earlier in this chapter, one can expect to see an increased attention to the fathers' effects upon daughters in the future.

One study relates the daughter's perception of the father's behavior to the daughter's ability to control cognitive performance in a somewhat stressful situation. Heilbrun, Harrell, and Gillard (1967) had categorized 123 female undergraduates into four groups according to whether they described their fathers as high or low in control and high or low in nurturing. In groups of five or less, each girl performed a task which required her to name the color of ink in which words were written. Each of these words was the name of a color other than the color it was written in. The experimenter said "wrong" and had the student correct herself each time she made an error. He explained that he was seeking to determine whether males or females were less distractible, and a monetary reward was offered for the best performance on the winning side. Paternally "rejected" females, those with fathers who were high in control and low in nurturance, had the largest number of errors. The best performances occurred in the "ignored" (low-control, low-nurturance) or "overprotected" (high-control, high-nurturance) groups, with the "accepted" (low-control, high-nurturance) falling in a middle position. The rank order of the groups was identical to what these authors had found when the mother's influence was considered. However, further analysis of the childrearing patterns of both parents indicated that the most descriptive pattern related to the daughter's cognitive performance was that of rejection by the father, while for mothers it was overprotection. Reasoning concerning the effects of rejection have centered on the effects of the consistent lack of approval of the child's behavior. As the present authors have defined rejection, an above-average level of control is combined with a below-average level of nurturance. This suggests that the rejecting father tended to direct or supervise his daughter's behavior while criticizing or withholding approval of the outcome. It isn't difficult to imagine how this type of pattern could affect the girl's competency in the experimental situation described.

Females are usually found to be more "field-dependent" than males. Field-dependence refers to the tendency to be more influenced by external cues in one's perception. Bieri (1960) reasoned that people who are identified with their fathers should show more independent, assertive, and active coping behaviors, the pattern corresponding to the field-independent person. He had thirty male and thirty female undergraduates take a measure of parental identification and the Embedded Figures Test, which is a measure of field dependence-independence. The females who were identified with the father made significantly fewer errors on the Embedded Figures Test, and thus were more field-independent than those who were identified with their mothers. The finding is consistent with the reasoning of several authors in this chapter that daughters may learn characteristics facilitative of active problem solving from fathers, depending on the nature of their relationship with their fathers.

There are several investigations linking the father's influence to some aspect of the sexual behavior of his daughter. In a survey of over 1,000 male and female students at sixteen coeducational colleges and universities, Winch (1950) found that high "courtship progress" was significantly more prevalent among females who thought their father loved them more than their mother did. It should be mentioned, incidentally, that the number of females who answered father (35) or mother (58) to the question, Which parent loves you more?, was small compared to the number who said they were undecided (409).

In an English study, Bene (1965) compared the early family relationships of thirty-seven homosexual women and eighty married women. The two groups were selected so that they were matched on ages, size of childhood families, and fathers' occupations so that the primary difference between the groups would be in sexual orientation. Of sixty-eight items on a questionnaire concerning early family relationships, twenty-four were answered differently concerning the father by the two groups, while only four were answered differently concerning the mother. In describing the father's behavior the homosexual women used the items expressing love and approval less often, and used items expressing hostility and disapproval more often, saw the father as more frightening, and described the father as lower in competence and strength of personality. In answer to questions concerning whether as a child they had wanted to become like either of the parents, 51 percent of the homosexual women had not wanted to be like their mothers and 54 percent had not wanted to be like their fathers. The results point more toward female homosexuality being linked to unsatisfactory relations between the daughter and a weak and incompetent father than toward the possibility of the female being homosexual because of overly strong identification with the father. It was also noted that 38 percent of the homosexual women as compared to 13 percent of the married women recalled that their parents had mentioned wanting a boy when the daughter had been born.

A study of twenty-four homosexual women by Kaye *et al.* (1967) describes the fathers as puritanical, exploitative, feared by the daughters, overly possessive, "subtly interested in his daughter physically," and tending to discourage her development as an adult. Fewer differences were found between the mothers of homosexual and nonhomosexual women. This study involved the questionable methodology of asking numerous psychoanalysts to fill out questionnaires concerning their homosexual and non homosexual patients who were in psychoanalytic treatment.

A comparison of fifty adult homosexual women with fifty adult heterosexual women indicates the differences between the fathers of the two groups were similar to the differences between the mothers of the two groups (Poole, 1972). The author was investigating the possibility that significant others "by gestures, overt behavioral manifestations and role model performance" during childhood shape the person's future erotic role behavior. For example, on a question concerning the mother's attitude toward sex, disapproval of sex was recalled as the attitude of 68 percent of the homosexual women's mothers as compared to only 28 percent of the mothers of heterosexual women. The comparable figures for fathers of the two groups were 60 percent and 32 percent. Forty-four percent of the mothers of homosexual women were described as lacking in affection and understanding, as compared to 10 percent of the mothers of heterosexual women. Again the pattern for fathers was similar with figures of 62 percent and 24 percent.

In discussing negative father-daughter influences some mention might be made of the relatively rare problem of incest (Cavallin, 1966; Maisch, 1972). Apparently in most countries the rate of convictions of fathers engaging in sexual behavior with their daughters runs around two cases per million in the population. The problem tends to occur at about the age of biological maturity in the daughter. It is apparently not the case that the majority of fathers involved are highly abnormal in intelligence or personality functioning. There is involved most often a disorganized family and a disturbed relationship between the husband and wife with their sexual relationship an unsatisfying one. The men usually evidence unstable personalities and lack of self-control, with an alcohol problem often part of the pattern. The victims tend to be very dependent on the father or stepfather, and have an unsatisfactory relationship with the mother or stepmother.

An illustration of
positive father-daughter influences

An illustration of the father's potentially strong and positive influence on his daughter is provided in Indira Priyadarshini Gandhi. As prime minister of India, the world's largest democracy and the country with the second largest population, she can be regarded as one of the most outstanding women of this century.

As Indira was growing up, her father, Jawaharlal Nehru, was active in the movement to gain India's independence from British rule. In their home she would wander into her father's meetings with other leaders active in the struggle. "Later she would gather the servants around and imitate the discussion she had heard," a clear example of the influence her father provided as a model. She was included in her father's travel and activities. When she was four she was held in her grandfather's arms during one of her father's trials. Indira's mother, Kamala Kaul, was also imprisoned for her part in the struggle. Indira's biographer, Rau (1966), comments:

> She was brought up in an atmosphere where higher duty to motherland was all that mattered in life. Everything else—personal feelings, affections, comforts—was to be sacrificed at this high altar. Her parents were a living example of it. (pp. 30-31)

This influence upon Indira had quite early results. When she was ten she traveled several miles by bicycle each week to work in a home for lepers. She regularly worked in slum areas. When she was twelve she formed a chidren's group of hand spinners. Presumably this was to help provide cloth locally and assist in the boycott of British goods. When she was sixteen she organized peers to help with routine duties of Congress Party men so that they could give more time to the movement for independence.

Though both parents provided strong examples the father's influence seems to have been particularly strong.

> Indira was not educated on conventional lines but the circumstances and personality of her father combined to give her one of the rarest educations that a person can acquire. Nehru took keen interest in her education and encouraged her to read and think for herself. While he was away, he carried on with the Great Dialogue through letters though he certainly did not consider it a satisfactory arrangement. (p. 33)

These letters were published in a book, *Letters from a*

Father to His Daughter. A sample of his writing to her when she was 13: "Never do anything in secret or anything that you would wish to hide, for the desire to hide anything means that you are afraid, and fear is a bad thing and unworthy of you. Be brave and all the rest follows." Certainly some other national leaders could have profited from such fatherly advice.

When Indira married Feroze Gandhi she wore a sari that her father wove while he was in prison. Later, when her son was only a few months old, she learned that her father was to be transferred between two prisons. She brought her son to a bridge over which her father would be driven. At dusk she held up his grandchild for him to see as he was driven across.

With India's independence and her father's election as Prime Minister, Indira served as his hostess, as his wife had died a few years earlier, and Indira also participated in policy making and vital decisions. Indira was later elected as Congress Party president, and still later, to the office of Prime Minister.

The evidence that the father can help to influence an effective instrumental, problem solving orientation in a daughter who is at the same time feminine, seems to be illustrated in the life of Indira Gandhi. Her comments in that area are of interest.

> Although I am in no sense a feminist, I happen to believe in the possibility of women being able to do everything.
>
> If a woman has qualifications and ability for any profession, she should be in it. A woman's work is more difficult than a man's because she has to look after her work as well as her home. I do not believe that a person who neglects the home can do other things well. (p. 79)

Summary

Current views of the development of female children depart considerably from the psychoanalytic view and its assumption that identification with the mother was the means by which a normal feminine girl acquired her characteristics. The research indicates that male and female parents respond differentially and uniquely to a male or a female child, and the responses of fathers may be the more specifically differentiated to the sex of the child. Normal daughters, relatively feminine for the most part, may acquire some of their characteristics through imitation of the father's characteristics. Acquisition of these characteristics may gain for the girl a wider, more adaptable range of behaviors than is true for the girl who closely resembles a very feminine mother.

5 fathers & children's development

Most of the research cited in the preceding chapters focuses on child-rearing effects of the father that differ from child-rearing effects of the mother, or effects of the father that differentiate between sons and daughters. Much of the research on the development of personality-social characteristics has focused on the role of parents in influencing the development of the characteristic, and the characteristics involved have been those for which the sex of the parent or child involved was of little significance. The findings often indicate that emphasis on some particular parent behavior is associated with and possibly causes strengthening of a certain behavior in the child.

As mentioned earlier, far too much of this research has been conducted only with the mothers in the study of the "parents." In cases where fathers have been included and it is possible to identify the effects of a particular behavior by either parent, we can learn of additional areas of child behavior that can be influenced by the father. Development of achievement motivation in the child appears to be one of these areas.

Achievement motivation refers to the ambition to do

well, relative to some standard of excellence. The person high in achievement motivation tends to work toward future goals rather than pursue immediate gratification, takes an active rather than a passive stance in influencing his position in life, favors individual achievement over stressing close involvement with his family, and takes moderate risks in order to achieve. Individuals' scores on measures of achievement motivation have been found to be moderately related to the individual's achievement on several indices that society notices, such as school grades, performance on aptitude and intelligence tests, level of education attained and status of the occupation the individual aspires to or attains (Byrne, 1974).

The parents of young boys measured as high in achievement motivation stressed early, independent task accomplishment for their children rather than greater indulgence (McClelland, 1953; Winterbottom, 1958; Cox, 1962). Specific tasks asked of the boys by their parents included knowing the way around the city or trying new things independently at an earlier age, and handling more household chores and responsibilities than was true for the boys lower in achievement motivation.

One particularly interesting study involved observing the mothers and fathers of both boys high in achievement motivation and boys low in achievement motivation, as the boys dealt with five different tasks in the presence of their parents in their own homes (Rosen & D'Andrade, 1959). Both groups of boys had been matched by age, race, IQ, and socioeconomic status, so that differences between them other than those due to achievement motivation would be minimized. Tasks such as one requiring the boy to form a hat rack using just two boards and a C clamp were intended to be somewhat stressful and frustrating in order to obtain from the parents more varied reactions than they would ordinarily show when "company" was present. The experimenters described the parents of boys high in achievement motivation as more interested in and concerned with their sons' performance. They had higher aspirations for their sons and tended to make the task more difficult for the boys in terms of the goals they suggested. The more highly motivated boys' parents reacted with more warmth and approval to their successes and particularly the mothers reacted with disapproval if the boys performed poorly. Some differences were also noted between the mothers and fathers of the boys high in achievement motivation (n Achievement). Mothers tended to push achievement training more than independence training and were more concerned with the boys' success.

> Fathers and mothers both provide achievement and independence training, but the fathers seem to contribute much more to the latter than do the mothers. Fathers tend to let their sons develop some self-reliance by giving hints . . . rather than always telling "how to do it." . . . They are less likely to push . . . and more likely to give the boy a greater degree of autonomy in making his own decision. Fathers of high n Achievement boys often appear to be competent men who are willing to take a back seat while their sons are performing. They tend to beckon from ahead rather than push from behind.
>
> The father who gives the boy a relatively high degree of autonomy provides him with an opportunity to compete on his own ground, to test his skill, and to gain a sense of confidence in his own competence. The dominating father may crush his son (and in so doing destroys the boy's achievement motive), perhaps because he views the boy as a competitor and is viewed as such by his son. (pp. 215-216)

Other findings have also pointed to differences in the male child's level of achievement motivation related to differences in just the father's behavior. One study of the male seventh- and eighth-graders in three different communities found the sons of fathers with entrepreneurial responsibility in their jobs to have achievement motivation scores about double those of sons whose fathers did not have such responsibility. This was true within either white or blue collar levels of occupation. Entrepreneurial aspects of an occupation included a high degree of autonomy, authority over two or more levels of subordinates, decision making obligations, and coordinating men and/or materials. Based on his own findings and those of others the author (Turner, 1970) speculated that the father's occupational activities would directly affect his behavior with his son.

> A father who is closely supervised, and who has little autonomy, decision-making power, or authority accumulates frustration leading to the expression of aggression in the family which cannot be expressed in the work place. . . . Conversely, a father who can exercise authority and who has autonomy and freedom on the job will be less frustrated and thus more likely to be nurturant and emphasize independence and mastery to his son. (p. 161)

Another channel of influence which the author could have suggested would be imitative learning, which might differ in the models provided by the two types of fathers. Dinner time conversation, for example, might involve a father from the entrepreneurial group describing decisions to pursue certain goals, while a son of the non-entrepreneurial group might hear his father describing the passive carrying out of what he was directed to do that day. The former instance would be the most likely to lead to a similar, active view of achieving goals in the observing son.

Cultural differences in the effects of fathers on their sons' achievement motivation were pointed out in a comparison between the United States and Turkey (Bradburn, 1963). Because fathers in Turkey tend to be more dominating and thus allow less autonomy for their sons, childhood separation from the father appears to be related to higher achievement motivation in the son, the reverse of the typical United States pattern. Fewer efforts have been made to understand the development of achievement motivation in girls, partly because there seemed to be little correspondence between the findings obtained with males and females at first. More recent research has indicated that the characteristics of female achievement motivation are more similar to the pattern for males the higher the educational level of the female (Baruch, 1967). The results also suggest that high achievement motivated females may express their motivation within their family of procreation, at least when numbers of younger children are at home (Littig and Yeracaris, 1965; Baruch, 1967).

Aggression

Although human aggression is a major social problem, one that in its more intense forms leads to many tragic acts of violence in our society each day, study of parental influence on its development has been limited. This may be in part because experimentation aimed at producing intense aggression in children would pose ethical problems. However, there are a number of correlational studies which focus on the differences in parental behavior in the background of children high or low in aggression.

In an intensive study of nursery school age children and their parents, Sears, Rau, and Alpert (1965) supported previous findings of higher levels of the more antisocial forms of aggression in boys, but they also point out that the more interpersonal, verbal, and prosocial forms (e.g., tattling) characterize girls. Probaly because it is antisocial aggression which poses the more obvious social problem, most studies of aggression have focused on male aggression.

Bandura and Walters (1959) studied antisocial aggression in twenty-six boys with no obvious sociological or constitutional disadvantages. The boys were average or above average in intelligence, and from unbroken homes in good neighborhoods, with their parents steadily employed. The boys and their parents were compared with a control group which matched the aggressive group in ages and the occupational rating of the father. The authors found that the aggressive boys felt less affection for their fathers than did the less aggressive boys, and the aggressive boys showed less identification with or preference for their fathers. Of possibly greater significance is the finding that both the fathers and the mothers of the aggressive boys encouraged them to show aggression outside the home, as indicated in the following interview:

> I. Has he ever come to you and complained that another fellow was giving him a rough time?
> F. Yes.
> I. What did you advise him to do about it?
> F. I told him to hit him.
> I. If Earl got into a fight with one of the neighbors' boys, how would you handle it?
> F. That would depend who was at fault. If my boy was at fault, he'd be wrong and I'd do my best to show him that. But if he was in the right I wouldn't want to chastise him.

I. How far would you let it go?

F. I'd let it go until one won. See who was the best man.

•••

I. have you ever encouraged Earl to stand up for himself?

M. Yes. I've taught young Earl, and his dad has. I feel he should stand up for his rights, so your can get along in this world.

I. How have you encouraged him?

M. I've told him to look after himself and don't let anybody shove him around or anything like that, but not to look for trouble. I don't want him to be a sissy.

I. Have you ever encouraged Earl to use his fists to defend himself.

M. Oh yes. Oh yes. He knows how to fight.

I. What have you done to encourage him?

M. When he was a little boy, he had a little pair of boxing gloves. His dad has been an athlete all his life, so his dad taught him.

Some of the fathers of the aggressive boys subtly encouraged their sons to show aggression against adults, as in the comment of one father, ". . . I've always encouraged Edward to stand up for himself when he's right regardless of the size of the other side." Again the message apparently was effective, as several of the aggressive boys had hit their teachers with fists or had thrown objects at them. Fathers of the less aggressive boys encouraged socially acceptable assertiveness in their sons, but usually discouraged physical aggression and would not allow their children to provoke other children.

Many experiments have shown that aggressive behavior examples observed by children can lead to increased aggression whether the models provided are "live" or in filmed or televised presentations (Bandura,

1973). Evidence that a more complex and delayed type of imitative learning may occur in families is provided in a study of thirty-four cases of child abuse (Silver, Dublin, and Lourie, 1969). The authors found records showing that some of the child abusers had been abused themselves as children, while many of the remaining cases illustrated other violence toward the abused child, abuse of the child's siblings, or abuse of one parent by the other.

An additional case that the authors refer to is that of Sirhan Sirhan, the assassin of Robert F. Kennedy, who was a United States Senator and candidate for the presidency:

> Teachers, pastors, and boyhood acquaintances who had known the subject in Jerusalem reported that he grew up in violence. Salim Awad, the headmaster of the Jerusalem Evangelical Lutheran School, was quoted as saying, "What the (school) records do not show is what went on at home. The father and mother had terrible fights and the children suffered as a result. Their father beat them."
>
> Pastor Daoud Haddad of the Lutheran Church of the Savior in Jerusalem stated that the father "had frequent violent fits and was given to breaking what little furniture they had, and beating the children. He thrashed them with sticks and with his fists whenever they disobeyed him."
>
> Salin Atas, a boyhood acquaintance of Sirhan, related an incident when the father heated an iron and pressed it against Sirhan's heel. "I remember Sirhan coming to school with no shoes." (p. 406)

As with most other behaviors there is more than one source of aggressive behavior patterns, and it cannot be concluded that the behavior of the father or of both parents is the general cause of aggression in the child. One must consider other factors such as the influence of television and other parts of the mass media, the response of the child's peers to aggression, and the child's size in relation to other children.

Competence

There is a recent series of studies by several different investigators, nominally focused on different characteristics, that fit together to show a pattern of parent behavior related to effective, self-confident behavior in children. Most of these have included information on the father, with resulting evidence for the effects of his influence. In addition, these studies serve to recommend particular styles of parent behavior that relate to a series of desirable characteristics in children.

The first of these studies to be described should probably be the one focused on the youngest age group. Baumrind (1967a, 1967b, 1970) has carefully observed the behavior of pre-school children in both their home and nursery school settings. She has linked the behavior of the children with their parents' behavior. She has assessed the latter both from observations of the parent-child interaction in the home and from interviews of the parents. The patterns of parent behavior and child characteristics that she has found to be related are as follows:

Parent Behavior	Child Characteristics
A. Controlling, demanding, communicative, and loving ("Authoritative")	A. Assertive, self-reliant, self-controlled
B. Controlling and detached ("Authoritarian")	B. Unhappy, disaffiliated
C. Noncontrolling, nondemanding, and relatively warm	C. Least self-reliant, least self-controlled

One of the most significant aspects of the father's behavior in Baumrind's findings (1967a) was the consistency of his discipline. Paternal consistent discipline was associated with likable, autonomous, imaginative, and confident behavior in boys, and well-socialized, friendly, and dependable behavior in girls. In this sample, which included some very highly educated fathers associated with a university, the fathers in the most highly educated group were the least consistent. The author speculated that these fathers might be too involved with their work to take a significant part in disciplining their children.

At about the same time that Baumrind's work on competence in nursery school children appeared, Coopersmith (1967) published work on self-esteem in pre-adolescent boys. Although the nominal focus of the two studies is different the child behavior involved and the parental behaviors correlated with it correspond closely. By self-esteem Coopersmith means "the evaluation which the individual makes and customarily maintains with regard to himself: it expresses an attitude of approval or disapproval, and indicates the extent to which the individual believes himself to be capable, significant, successful, and worthy. In short, self-esteem is a *personal* judgment of worthiness that is expressed in the attitudes the individual holds toward himself."

Coopersmith determined the self-esteem of fifth- and sixth-grade boys both from their self-ratings and from their teachers' ratings of apparent self-esteem in the boys, though he relied mainly on the former measure. By a wide range of situational, questionnaire, and interview measures, the boys who were higher in self-esteem were found to represent a better level of adjustment than was true for the boys who were medium or low in self-esteem. The boys high in self-esteem were more resistant to pressure to conform to incorrect judgments of their peers, were less sensitive to the disapproval of other people, were more often leaders rather than listeners in group discussions, and were more likely to be selected as friends by their classmates. The high self-esteem boys were less concerned with inner problems, were able to devote more attention to broader problems of the world and were more creative. The high self-esteem boys were described by their mothers as having fewer "mental health" problems, fewer physical symptoms of the type that are largely psychosomatic, and as being least destructive. From these and other considerations it seems clear that the high self-esteem child represents the outcome most people would want in their children, and is quite similar to the competent child of Baumrind's study.

In studying what background factors of these boys were related to their levels of self-esteem, Coopersmith found little importance in the socioeconomic status, intelligence, or attractiveness of the boys. The main relationships were in interactions with other people, particularly the characteristics of family interaction.

A fairly clear pattern of parental behavior was related to high self-esteem. These parents were relatively strict, thought it was more important for the boy to meet high standards than to enjoy himself, and enforced rules more firmly and consistently. Yet the parents favored reward for the child's successes rather than punishment for his failures. When punishment was used it was not likely to be corporal punishment, but rather restraint, denial, or isolation. The parents of the high self-esteem boy were most favorable toward the child having a voice in the making of family plans, deciding his own bedtime, and questioning the thinking of his parents. These parents were most likely to stress discussion and reason-

ing rather than force, and autocratic means to obtain the
child's cooperation or compliance. Coopersmith speculates that higher self-esteem may result from several
aspects of this pattern, including the fact that clear
parental standards are provided by which the child can
judge his own behavior and know where he stands, and
that within broad firm limits the child is given freedom
to assert himself. Of considerable significance also may
be the parental expectations that the child will perform
as competently as he can.

Although fathers were not even questioned directly
in this study many aspects of the father's behavior as
reported by the mother or as evident in the demographic
information were related to the son's self-esteem. The
findings reported above are in many cases based on
descriptions by the mother or son of the behavior of both
parents. In addition there were several indications of
differences between the fathers of lower and higher
esteem boys. In the families of the high self-esteem boys
52 percent of them indicated their father was the person
in whom they would be most likely to confide, as
compared to 15 and 17 percent of the medium and low
self-esteem subjects. The mothers of high and medium
self-esteem boys were more pleased with the father's
performance in rearing the child than was true in the low
self-esteem cases. The fathers of boys of high self-esteem
and the fathers of boys whose self-ratings were close to
the teachers' ratings of the boys' self-esteem, were the
most likely to be regularly employed, seldom absent for
job-related reasons, and stable and secure in their positions. The fathers of the high self-esteem boys tended to
have the highest aspirations for their sons' future work
status.

Additional support for the connection between this

particular pattern of parent behavior and desirable
results in children's personalities comes from the report
of a study sponsored by the U. S. Department of Labor
(Glaser & Ross, 1970). Thirty-two successful and thirty-
eight unsuccessful young men in the Los Angeles area
were studied. The successful young men were those who
had been working or going to school on their own more
or less steadily in the last two years, had not been on
welfare in the last two years, and had not been in serious
trouble with the law in recent adulthood. About half of
each group were black, and half were Mexican-
American. All had grown up in a large city ghetto and
had been disadvantaged with regard to housing, food,
and/or clothing. No difference was found between the
successful and unsuccessful groups on a nonverbal intelligence test. The question was, of course, if the young
men all started from a disadvantaged background with
similar ability, what made the difference between those
who were successful and those who were not. Young men
from the ethnic origin and background of the subjects
conducted interviews with them to find out.

Many of the findings were similar in either Mexican-
American or black families. The families of the
successful men were recalled as warm and supportive.
They described parents who were effective in setting
standards, and consistent and effective in their discipline.
The successful young men had the impression that their
parents had expected them to succeed academically and
occupationally. The successful young men found school
a pleasant experience. They achieved some academic
success and formed important relationships with
teachers and coaches. Most of these men had long-range
and realistic goals they were pursuing and they derived a
positive self-esteem from their accomplishments. These

findings all fell in the opposite direction for the unsuccessful young men.

A key difference between the two ethnic groups was related to the role of the father. In the Mexican-American family, absence of the father was synonymous with lack of effective standards and control for the boy's behavior. The authors related this to the Mexican-American culture's expectation that the mother should continue to give love and support to her children without its being conditional on the child's behavior. Only the father or his surrogate should make demands concerning the behavior standards of the boy. This difference did not characterize the black families, where the effective parent was as likely to be the mother as the father.

A fourth aspect of personality appears to overlap with the concepts of competence, high self-esteem, and successfulness. This aspect is referred to as internal-external locus of control, and the name refers to the differences in where individuals tend to locate the control for events that occur to them. One child does poorly on a test and concludes that he did not prepare well enough, so the control over the event is seen by him as internal. A second child who does poorly may attribute the outcome to the unfairness of the teacher in asking the questions on the test, so the control is external to the child. People who tend to believe in internal control seem to react in a more active, problem-solving manner in a variety of situations such as in school achievement, response to reports of the link between smoking and cancer, and involvement in social action (MacDonald, 1971; Strickland, 1965).

Crandall (1973) studied the antecedents of internal-external control by relating data on parental behavior toward the research subjects during childhood to their control orientation in adulthood. She obtained the childhood data on these sixty-five people from the Fels longitudinal study. Repeated observations of these children and their parents had been recorded during their childhood. She found that the adults with an internal control orientation had mothers who "pushed their children toward greater independence, less often rewarded dependency, and displayed less intense involvement and contact with them."

> But why, theoretically, should this push and encouragement to 'leave the nest' be so helpful in the establishment of internal perceptions? I would like to suggest that its function is to put the child into more active intercourse with his physical and social environment so that there is more opportunity for him to observe the effect of his own behavior, the contingency between his own action and ensuing events, unmediated by maternal intervention. (p. 13)

Though these parental characteristics were derived from actual observations of the parents, it is interesting that the internal-control adults describe their parents as less hostile, detached, and/or rejecting. Perhaps this indicated that in the long run the children saw the "push out of the nest" as positive behavior by their parents.

While Crandall's findings were based on study of the mother's behavior only, she notes that the findings for the father's influence are on the whole similar in nature. For example, MacDonald (1971) related university students' reports of male and female parent behavior to the internal-external control orientation of the students. He found that a greater internal-control orientation of the students of both sexes was associated with the reported parental behaviors of high maternal and paternal nurturance, low maternal protectiveness toward the child, and high maternal predictability of standards. An additional finding for male students was that greater internal control was associated with more paternal physical punishment, which is a puzzling finding unless it too is an indication of high standards for the boy's behavior being enforced by the father.

An example of development of internal control

A family which seems to illustrate an unusually high degree of belief in internal control, and competent, problem solving behavior, is that of the Naders. Much of what they have done seems to illustrate achievement motivation with an altruistic goal rather than the goal of personal financial gain so common in our society. Rather than echo the cliche "You can't fight city hall," they have done so and won.

Most familiar is Ralph Nader, known around the world for his many struggles and victories focused on protecting the interests and welfare of the ordinary person in his "consumption" of the products of governments and corporations (McCarry, 1972). Laura Nader, Ralph's older sister, is a full professor in the anthropology of law at the University of California, Berkeley (Another Nader, 1970). Her work focuses on a critical review of the United States legal system as compared to the systems of other cultures. Shaffak Nader, Ralph's older brother, led campaigns to keep parking meters off the streets of their home town, and to establish a community college (*Meet Ralph Nader*, 1968).

The father of this group, Nathra Nader, is an immigrant from Lebanon who came to the United States with little money, returned to Lebanon to marry, and then returned to the United States to start his family and

a restaurant. Many observations about the father suggest
the kind of influence evident in the children:

> "The Highland Arms (the Nader restaurant) was no
> place to go and eat in peace," says Mrs. Claire Vrie-
> land, who still lives in Winsted. "Mr. Nader would
> always try to heat everybody up about wrongs and
> iniquities. If someone strange was in town you'd send
> them there because it was nearby and decent. They'd
> come back with indigestion and berate you. Mr. Nader
> would never let anything alone." (McCarry, p. 32)
>
> "Conditions in the country were always talked over
> by us and we talked it over with the children," Nathra
> Nader says. "We asked why; we expected them to ask
> why too." (p. 33)
>
> And I also told the children, "Don't ever look up to
> anyone, or look down on anyone. We don't think any
> person is bigger than us or that we are any bigger than
> you are." (*Meet Ralph Nader*, 1968, p. 70)

Laura notes that her father often led the family in
evening discussions about "hypothetical and real problems in society and what should be done about them." As
might be expected Rose Nader, the mother, was similar
in her influence. Laura comments:

> We used to come home from school for lunch and
> my mother would have a "historical serial" on some
> aspect of world history. Every day she'd give us a new
> chapter at lunch. My parents believe the education of
> children begins at home.

The mother's views on raising children sound close
to the recommendations one would draw from Coopersmith's work on self-esteem referred to above.

> "I believe how to bring up a child is to give the child
> self-confidence and courage," Mrs. Nader says. "He
> must speak up when it's time to do so. The child

should also listen; you must teach him how to listen."
(McCarry, p. 37)

Ralph Nader's biographer points out both the
family closeness and cultural uniqueness that helped the
Naders not to fall into the passive conformity typical of
our society:

> The Naders were Greek Orthodox Catholics who
> went to the Methodist Sunday school, property owners
> who did not belong to the Yankee establishment,
> foreigners even to the town's large Italian population,
> were closely bound together because there was no other
> family quite like them. "They weren't part of the usual
> world," says a Winsted man, "so they never feared the
> world. You could maybe say they just went ahead
> because they didn't know what couldn't be done."
> (McCarry, p. 32)

Creativity is another desirable characteristic of children, and one that is linked at least partially to intellectual ability. The indications so far are that significant
creative accomplishment is rare in those with anything
less than average intelligence (Dellas and Gaier, 1970).
Above that limitation there is evidence that the behavior
of parents can influence the degree of creativity in their
children.

One interesting study (Bishop and Chace, 1971)
focused on the role of both parents in establishing a
home play environment encouraging to creativity in
three- and four-year-old children. It was found that
"abstract" mothers who encouraged flexibility, exploration, and autonomy in their children's play had children
of greater creative potential, but the father's behavior
showed little relationship to creative potential in this
study.

In a study of fifty highly intelligent children (Weisberg and Springer, 1967) those who scored higher in creativity were found to be from somewhat different types of families than those who scored lower in creativity. The family of the more creative child was described as one with open and not always calm expression of feelings and less stress on conformity to parental values. The father was described as strongly and positively involved with the child. He was described as a man of some authority both at work and at home but not dominating. The mother was described as interacting strongly with the child but tending to be ambivalent in her maternal feelings. The picture of the families was based on psychological tests and on interviews with the parents and children.

Ravenna Helson has obtained information about parents in several studies of creativity. In a study of 135 creative college women (1967, 1968) the author found the creative students to have had relationships of about equal intensity with both the father and mother. The fathers were described as gentle and controlled, characteristics which may have made them more available as models for their daughters. Both parents were described as having intellectual or artistic interests, and the fathers in particular were described as men of principle or moral integrity. The information was obtained from a wide variety of measures used with the creative women and their families, and from interviews with the creative women.

In a similar study of thirty-four creative mathematicians the same author (Helson and Crutchfield, 1970) found some evidence that characteristics of the mother distinguish the creative from the average mathematician, but that the characteristics of the father were related to the type of creativity of the mathematician.

Anne Roe (1953) studied the backgrounds of many of

the foremost American research scientists. She found that the influence of the fathers varied to some extent depending on the science involved. Great respect for the father was characteristic of the physical scientists, but the social scientists described more conflict with their families. While only 3 percent of the employed men in the country were professionals, the author found that 53 percent of the fathers of the scientists were professionals. The following remarks from one of the theoretical physicists are a bit unusual in the closeness apparent between the father and son, but are representative of the respect or influences on particular interests in many of the father-son relationships in Roe's study.

> Father never even got through high school and started at practically hard labor at thirteen and got from that to be a star salesman. I don't know when he found time for the things he did. He was quite athletic and at that time there were amateur athletic groups and he was stroke. I never realized how good he was at the time but later I found some old papers and found that his crew was the best anywhere around. All the training was done after a day's work. Then some time later some of the books I read when I was a kid were some International Correspondence School texts on engineering which he had studied. That's a lot of work when you are working hard too. Father was a better man than I was or ever will be. Even when I was young and strong my father was much stronger and tougher than I was always. (pp. 118-119)

> Father had a strong mechanical bent and I learned quite a bit from him without realizing it. From the age of ten or so I was entrusted with keeping his car serviced. By the time I was 12 there were several of us interested in radio and we made a set. (p. 119)
> . . . if I asked him how to do something he always knew and he had tools around which he got for his

own purposes. . . . He never gave me any formal instruction but I learned a lot. (p. 120)

Children's attitudes on several topics have been shown to be reflections of those of the parents. While it might be that one or the other parent might typically have the most influence on a child's attitudes, the approach of most researchers has been to use an indication of "parental" attitudes, apparently assuming that most husbands and wives would be in fairly close agreement. The findings from this research then suggest that the father is a joint influence on the attitudes of his children.

There has been considerable interest in trying to understand the development of attitudes of prejudice toward people who are different in race, religion, or other characteristics. Epstein and Momorita (1966a) had 180 third- to fifth-grade children view slides of a (fictitious) people called "Piraneans." For different groups of children the people in the slides were either white, oriental, or black. After viewing the slides the children were asked to indicate how closely they would accept these people on a social distance scale ranging from, "Would you want these people to visit your country?" to "Would you want to marry these people when you grow up?" Similar questions were answered by the children concerning their acceptance of Germans, French, Catholics, Italians, Mexicans, Negroes, Japanese, Jews, and Russians. Three weeks later the children filled out the social distance scales concerning the same series of peoples as the children thought their parents would rate the groups. The children's nonacceptance of black or oriental Piraneans was found to correlate (.61) with their impressions of their parents' nonacceptance of blacks or orientals, and less strongly (.35) with their impressions of parental nonacceptance of the religious or national origin groups. The children's prejudice toward the eight groups was not significantly correlated with their descriptions of their parents' punitiveness, as would have been predicted from the more psychodynamic explanation of prejudice based on study of the authoritarian personality, an alternative explanation for the development of prejudice.

When the same authors did a related study with black children in Detroit (Epstein and Komorita, 1966b), their findings were quite similar to those of the previous study. The prejudice of the black children toward black Piraneans was significantly correlated (.40 to .67) with their impressions of their parents' nonacceptance of ten groups of differing religions and national origins. The children's attitudes toward the ten groups correlated closely (.73) with their impressions of parental attitudes toward the same groups.

A similar study looked at the attitudes of English-Canadian children toward English-speaking and French-speaking people (Gardner, Taylor, and Feenstra, 1970). Responses were obtained from 111 fourteen- to fifteen-year-old children, and questionnaires were sent home to be answered by the father if possible, or if not, by the mother. The authors found that these teenagers had a marked similarity to their parents on generalized authoritarian attitudes, although the specific attitudes involved in their stereotypes of French-speaking people were less related to those of the parents. In a subsequent study (Kirby and Gardner, 1972) the authors looked at stereotypes about English Canadians, French Canadians, and Canadian Indians in children of three age levels (nine-ten, eleven-thirteen, fourteen-seventeen) and their parents. They found that, with the exception of attitudes toward Canadian Indians, older children's stereotypes were more like those of the adults.

The book *Children's Views of Foreign Peoples* (Lambert and Klineberg, 1967) describes an interview study of 3300 children in eleven nations around the world. In most countries the six-year-old children described their views about people of other countries as having come from their parents. However, the ten- and fourteen-year-old children attributed increasing amounts of influence to television programs, movies, school classes, books, and other sources with the parents being mentioned very little as the basis for the views of the fourteen-year-olds.

Greenstein (1965) in his book *Children and Politics* describes his study of political attitudes in 659 fourth- to eighth-grade children in Connecticut. He found that as early as the fourth grade over 60 percent of the children could state their party preference, although by the eighth grade fewer than half could describe any differences between the political parties on issues. The party preference of the children mimicked that of their parents in practically every instance. While the author did not attempt to determine the relative influence of each parent in determining the young child's initial political preference, he did report that both young and adult females were less involved in the range of political activities, so it is possible that this parental influence comes primarily from the father. If this research were repeated today, of course, there might be a somewhat higher level of political concern and activity evident in the females than there was earlier.

At one point many people might have questioned whether parental influence on their offspring's attitudes, especially in the political area, was any longer in effect.

Particularly near the end of the 1960s, with rebellion on many campuses and young people marching through the streets to protest the Vietnam War and related political policies of the older generation, the mass media spent much time focusing on the "generation gap." However, it may be that this gap occurred in comparing only some young people to some parts of the older generation. Flacks (1967) studied protesters, activists, nonactivists, and antiprotesters on the University of Chicago campus, as well as many of their parents. In general the "gap" appeared much larger between families of different political attitudes than between different generations of the same family. Flacks found, "only six percent of nonactivists' fathers were willing to describe themselves as 'highly liberal' or 'socialist,' whereas sixty percent of the activists' [sic] fathers accepted such designations." The pattern is shown in the attitudes Flacks found on particular issues:

	Activists		Nonactivists	
Percent who approve	Students	Fathers	Students	Fathers
Bombing of North Vietnam	9	27	73	80
Student participation in protest demonstrations	100	80	61	37
Lyndon Johnson	35	77	81	83
Socialization of the medical profession	94	43	30	27

Byrne (1965) conducted a study that reveals the influence of both parents in attitude formation. The F scale was administered to 108 university students as a measure of authoritarian attitudes, and the Traditional Family Ideology Scale, a measure of authoritarian attitudes in child-rearing and family relationships, was administered to their parents. The two scales usually correlate fairly highly. However, correlating the Traditional Family Ideology Scale scores of male and female parents with the F scores of male and female students yielded only one correlation large enough to be statistically significant, and that was for the father-son combination. Stronger relationships resulted from considering the attitudes of both parents. Authoritarian offspring were most likely to develop in families in which neither parent was low in authoritarianism and the same-sex parent was high in authoritarianism. Conversely, equalitarian offspring were most likely to come from families in which at least one parent was low in authoritarianism and the same sex parent was not high in authoritarianism.

Elkind (1961) found that the child's religious orientation in the initial stage (five-six years old) was often a direct reflection of his parents' orientation and often preceded any understanding of the differences among religious groups. His results were obtained from several hundred Jewish, Catholic, and Protestant children. Some examples of the comments of the children at different ages follow:

(6yrs. 5mos.)   How do you become a Jew? . . . "Your father is Jewish so you must be Jewish." (p. 218)
(9yrs. 4mos.)   "Your parents are Jewish so you are Jewish." (p. 219)
(8yrs. 11mos.) What is a Protestant? "He belongs to a Protestant family." (p. 294)

Some responses indicated the wide reach of parental influence.

(8yrs. 4mos.)   Can a dog or a cat be a Protestant? "Yes." Why? "Because everybody in our house is Christian." (p. 294)

The final area of general paternal influences on

children to be considered is that of abnormal behavior. Schizophrenia, the psychotic disorder which fills most of the mental hospital beds, is a particularly interesting part of this topic. Schizophrenia seems to be such a multifaceted disorder that investigators with widely differing theories about its origin in individuals have been able to find support for their pet theories.

In many of the early investigations the "schizophrenogenic" mother was singled out as the cause of the disorder. Some authors suggested that the blame fell on the mother in the family of the schizophrenic because her obviously "eccentric and paralogic" characteristics impressed the psychiatrist she harassed, and because this was a reasonable theoretical conclusion based upon (psychoanalytic) theoretical considerations focusing on the patient's early years (Lidz, Parker, and Cornelison, 1956). As a series of investigations focused more broadly on the schizophrenic person and his family, it became apparent that the fathers were influential enough to share the blame for what were usually blatantly abnormal family patterns (Lidz, Parker, and Cornelison, 1956; Lidz and Fleck, 1960; Ellison and Hamilton, 1949; Eisenberg, 1957; McKeown and Chyatte, 1972; Da Silva, 1963; Wolman, 1970).

Wolman, in the *Manual of Child Psychopathology* (1972), summarizes many findings when he says, "The schizogenic family relationship represents a *reversal of social positions* which creates in the child, who eventually becomes schizophrenic, a confusion regarding social roles of age, sex, and family position." He notes that no mother could "destroy her child without the active or tacit assistance of her husband, and all fathers of schizophrenics participate in producing schizophrenia in their children."

TABLE 1
BEHAVIOR OF FATHERS AS RELATED TO
DIAGNOSTIC GROUP OF MALE AND FEMALE CHILDREN*

	FATHER: Demanding Antagonistic	FATHER: Superficial	FATHER: Encouraging	FATHER: Protective-Indulgent	Total
FEMALE					
Normals	15	32	70	8	125
Neurotics	28	17	9	2	56
Schizophrenics	27	35	11	6	79
					260
MALE					
Normals	28	62	70	7	167
Neurotics	12	7	8	2	29
Schizophrenics	26	26	21	5	78
					274

* Adapted from McKeown and Chyatte, 1954.

The apparent reversal of usual roles had been noticed in the behavior of schizophrenics in the hospital (McClelland and Watt, 1968). Female schizophrenics are usually more assertive than normal women, their wards are noisier than male wards, while male schizophrenics are usually more sensitive and quiet.

Kayton and Biller (1970) asked twenty each of normal, neurotic, paranoid schizophrenic and nonparanoid schizophrenic men to sort fifteen descriptive paragraphs as to whether the traits described were more typical of their mothers or fathers. Characteristics such as achievement, aggression, and endurance are usually attributed to males while others such as affiliation and nurturance are attributed more often to females. The normals were the most likely to see their parents as differing in the usual directions on the characteristics, while neurotics and schizophrenics perceived fewer systematic differences between their parents. This kind of observation may partly explain the atypical sex roles of schizophrenic patients.

Ellison and Hamilton (1949) mention an interesting example of sex role reversal in one father and some of the later problems of his son.

> One such father, husband of a woman self-described as "boss of the home," was banished to the kitchen whenever company called and had been reduced to a menial position in the family business. His son proved impotent on his wedding night and nearly succeeded in committing suicide. (p. 455)

The son was later hospitalized as a schizophrenic.

It should be noted that the apparent sex-role reversal in some schizophrenics should not be overemphasized. McClelland and Watt (1968) point out that the parent's behavior may have the effect of alienating the child from his usual role. This may mean reacting like the opposite-sex because that is the only alternative in some parts of behavior.

Wolman (1970), who has studied 160 cases of schizophrenia, has found about 40 percent of fathers and 30 percent of the mothers to have "a great variety of pathological conditions." His figures suggesting that the father is more frequently disturbed than the mother are interesting in view of earlier assumptions of the mother's singular significance in influencing the disorder. However, he found it impossible to specify particular types of parents that would cause schizophrenia in their offspring. There are some general inadequacies of parental functioning that he points to:

> The parents of schizophrenic children do not offer guidance and control. They fail to reinforce clear concepts of time and space because their own life is disorganized. They offer no reward or punishment, nor do they meet the child's need for gratification. They communicate in a confusing manner and give conflicting instructions. . . . (p. 46)

This description contrasts markedly with the pattern described earlier in the chapter as relating to more positive behaviors such as high self-esteem, competence, and internal locus of control.

Wolman describes some of the specific behaviors shown by the fathers:

> Many of these fathers resent being fathers and compete with their preschizophrenic children for the favors of their wives. One father was competing and fighting with his daughter at the dinner table for an additional serving of dessert.
>
> One father used to display his drugs and medicines whenever his child was sick as if to say, "I am sicker than you." Another father did not approach the bed of his sick child out of fear of contagion. When a preschizophrenic child boasted his success in foreign

language studies, his father started to study Latin to
show his wife that he could master a more difficult
language than his son did.

When a preschizophrenic girl broke her leg and was
brought home by neighbors, the irate father slapped
her face for what she was doing to him (i. e., forcing
him to take care of her).

Many fathers indulged in sexual activities with their
daughters and several of them hugged, kissed, and
petted their teen-age daughters. (p. 59)

A father of an autistic four-year-old boy was as
remarkable for his uninvolvement with his children as
the previous examples are for the destructive involvement of the father (Kanner and Eisenberg, 1955).

The father, a busy surgeon, was a perfectionist and a
detached individual who spent his vacations all by
himself and boasted that he never wasted his time
talking to his patients and their relatives. When asked
specifically, he was not quite sure whether he would
recognize any of his three children if he met them on
the street; he did not resent the question and its
obvious implication. (p. 234)

In a study of the histories of fifty male and female
patients who had become schizophrenic before the age of
twenty-one, Lidz and Lidz (1949) found that extreme
instability of the parents was evident in the mother in
nine cases, the father in eight, and both parents in six.
Noting this and other indications that the father is often
as much a part of the disturbed background of the
schizophrenic as the mother is, these authors were among
the earliest to observe, "had there been a stable father to
offer guidance or to serve as a source for stable identification, the patient would not have been so seriously
affected by the mother's difficulties."

The following table from a comparison of

schizophrenic and control group young males shows the difference between the fathers' behavior in the two groups (Gerard and Siegel, 1950):

	Schizophrenics		Controls	
	Number	**Percent**	**Number**	**Percent**
No father present after age two	5	7.1	0	0
Disinterested father, little contact	35	50.0	2	6.7
Interested father, little contact	21	35.7	8	26.7
Interested father, good contact	5	7.1	20	66.6
Data not available for judgment	1	0	0	0

The other side of the "little contact" characteristic of the fathers was a "markedly heightened relationship with the mother" for 91.4 percent of the schizophrenics and none of the control group males. Clear dominance of the mother in the family was true for 66.2 percent of the schizophrenics and 33 percent of the controls.

Cheek (1965) took a more systematic look at the father's part in the families of schizophrenics by analyzing the participation of each of the parents and the schizophrenic person as they discussed family-relations problems on which they were in disagreement. The author obtained four recorded discussions from each of sixty-seven families with young adult schizophrenics and fifty-six families with nonpsychotic young adults. The behavior of the fathers differed somewhat depending on the sex of the patient. The fathers of male schizophrenics were less active and made fewer procedural suggestions in the discussions than was true for the fathers of normals. This fits with the "passive, ineffectual father" often noted in previous research. The fathers of female schizophrenics had higher rates of total activity and normal rates of procedural suggestions, perhaps fitting the "proud, narcissistic father" sometimes noted by previous studies of female schizophrenics. Cheek also noted the smaller than normal sex-role differentiation between the parents of schizophrenics, and the fact that the male patients were passive and withdrawn as compared to the normal boys, while the females were overactive and dominating as compared to the normal girls.

Unfortunately, then, fathers seem to be as significant as mothers in contributing inadequate parental behavior to the set of factors involved in the development of schizophrenia. The earlier focus on the "schizogenic" or "schizophrenogenic mother" overlooked apparently equally destructive effects stemming from the father's behavior.

As might be expected from the difficulty researchers have had in finding a single pattern of parent inadequacies in the childhood of schizophrenics, many of the undesirable behavior patterns shown by the fathers of schizophrenics are noted in the childhood of people with other types of disorders. For example, more cross-sexed or less distinctively masculine behavior is noted in the fathers of neurotics than for the fathers of normal males (Rabkin, 1964; Kayton and Biller, 1970) as was true for schizophrenic cases. Fathers of neurotics and children with conduct disorders are described as variously more punitive, demanding, and antagonistic, or as superficial, weak, and ineffectual (McKeown and Chyatte, 1954; Rabkin, 1964; Peterson, Becker, Hellmer, Shoemaker and Quay, 1959). Both the mothers and fathers of six- to twelve-year-old problem children referred to clinics were judged "less well adjusted and sociable, more autocratic, and to experience more disciplinary contention" than was true for parents of a nonclinic control group (Peterson, Becker, Hellmer, Shoemaker, and Quay, 1959).

One effort was aimed at determining the particular types of father-child relationships (FCR's) that were correlated with specific problems of children (Rosenthal, Ni, Finkelstein, and Berkwits, 1962). They studied 406 cases of five- to fourteen-year-old children with emotional problems. The majority of children were male. The correspondence that they found between FCR's and the child's problems is shown in Table 2. The FCR's can be fairly well understood from the category titles used in the table, except that pushing to early responsibility involved expecting more mature behavior than that appropriate to the child's level of development, punitive refers to severe punishment that was not always physical, and the cold, distant, neglectful category included some fathers whose work caused them to be absent from the home a great deal. The only problem showing some relationship to a reasonably wholesome FCR was that of overly conforming or submissive behavior in the child. In the other FCR's those involving hostility of the father toward the child were linked with antisocial behavior such as stealing and temper problems. The authors note that these antisocial problems constitute evidence of the ineffectiveness of those fathers in controlling the behavior of their children. In the cold, distant, neglectful or controlling, rigid FCR's involving less overt hostility from the father, the child's problems were of a more neurotic inhibitory variety. Except for stealing, the problems related to the FCR of pushing to early responsibility indicated assertive behavior on the part of the child.

TABLE 2
PATTERN OF FATHER-CHILD RELATIONSHIPS AS RELATED TO THE PRESENCE OF PROBLEMS IN CHILDREN.*

Child's Problems	FATHER-CHILD RELATIONSHIPS						
	Reasonably Wholesome	Controlling, Rigid	Pushing to Early Responsibility	Punitive	Cold, Distant, Neglectful	Conflicting Authorities	Undetermined, Not Applicable
1. Temper				+c		+d	
2. Stealing, solitary	-a	+b	+b	+d	+c	+c	
3. Truancy		+a		+d			-a
4. Disobedient, hostile			+b	+c		+b	
5. Disobedient, mild or unspecified					+b		
6. Lying		+c		+c	+c	+c	
7. Destructiveness				+c	+a		
8. Learning defect, or progress unsatisfactory							
9. Bullying, domineering, aggressive			+b	+c		+a	

	Item					
10.	Victimized, teased				+c	
11.	Withdrawn, seclusive, daydreaming	-a				
12.	Generally immature					
13.	Overly competitive with siblings					+c
14.	Overly competitive with others		+a	+a		
15.	Depressed, discouraged	-b	+a	+c		+d
16.	Restless, excitable		+b	+b		+c
17.	Shy					
18.	Chronically anxious or fearful				+b	
19.	Reluctance or fear of school					
20.	Overly conforming, submissive	+c				

FATHER-CHILD RELATIONSHIPS

Child's Problems	Reasonably Wholesome	Controlling, Rigid	Pushing to Early Responsibility	Punitive	Cold, Distant, Neglectful	Conflicting Authorities	Undetermined, Not Applicable
21. Peculiar actions, delusions, compulsions, obsessions, phobias, etc.							+b
22. Frequent nightmares			-b			+a	
23. Enuresis, fixation							
24. Enuresis, regression				+c		+c	
25. Nailbiting					-b		
26. Thumbsucking							
27. Speech defects				+a			
28. Feeding problems							
29. Sleep disturbances							

Code for X^2 values: a, significant at < 0.10 level; b, significant at < 0.05 level; c, significant at < 0.01 level; d, significant at < 0.001 level; - indicates correlation would be negative.
*Adopted from Rosenthal, Ni, Finkelstein, and Berkwitz, 1962.

The authors note that instead of viewing these correlational relationships as indicating that the father's behavior toward the child contributed to the child's problems, one could argue that the child's behavior resulted in the father's reactions. That is, a child might first begin stealing and the father might become punitive in response. Often it is clear that this is not so in particular cases since parental behavior patterns have been fairly consistent over many years and several children. However, the child-to-parent direction of influence may be quite important in particular cases, and no doubt contributes to the patterns of parent behavior in many cases so that a "vicious circle" is maintained.

The study of psychosomatic disorders in children has typically involved a focus on the mother-child relationship, but the area has yielded some indications of the father's contribution to the problem. One study of the psychosomatic aspects of asthma concludes that in the cases where there is very little physical predisposition, one of the psychological factors evident is that the wife excludes the husband from the mother-child relationship, the wife has become more domineering and aggressive during the marriage, and the husband is considered irresponsible by the wife (Block, Jennings, Harvey, and Simpson, 1964). An obvious question about such a conclusion concerns the extent to which it is correct to view the mother as the active person in bringing about the state of parent-child relationships described. Can one adult in the family be excluded if he does not tacitly agree to cooperate with the exclusion? Such conclusions may point to both the frequent bias of researchers in focusing on mother-child relationships and at the same time suggest the nature of the father's role in the background of these children.

Two other investigators found the child's perception of the father to be a key difference between children with more or less of a physiological basis for their asthma (Baraff and Cunningham, 1965). The children with less of a physiological basis for their asthma described their fathers as less nice, less powerful, and less active than themselves.

Ulcers in children are fortunately a relatively rare problem, but there are a few studies such as one focusing on eight children, most of whom had ulcers or other gastrointestinal disorders (Mohr, Richmond, Garner, and Eddy, 1955). In this group a couple of the fathers were described as fairly adequate, but uninvolved with the family. Of the remainder four were alcoholics, and one was brutal and abusive, and neglected his family to the point of starvation.

Another study was of six boys from seven to fifteen years of age who had duodenal ulcers (Taboroff and Brown, 1954). In five of the families there was a history of long-time chaos. In the sixth there was parental stability but the mother had been in the hospital repeatedly during the boy's first seven years. Much of the instability of the five families was related to the fathers. One father had died in combat, two were divorced, and in these three families there were now stepfathers. Three of the fathers had ulcers themselves. One father had frequently threatened to shoot the son and mother.

This writer attempted to help one family which was probably representative of the situations in which children develop ulcers. The child with ulcers was a bright ten-year-old boy, whom we shall call Jerry. His father was a professional who was probably competent in his field, but was less than adequate in his ability to deal with people. The mother was a housewife without significant problems, except that she was unambitious and not a likely alternate model for the son. For a couple of decades this couple had had arguments on most evenings. The mood was typically tense whenever the family was together. The conflict between the parents often disappeared as soon as they went to bed, but this different aspect of their relationship was unknown to Jerry and not of comfort to him. His father would go away for professional meetings and other activities which sometimes involved six-to-eight-week absences every couple of years. While the mother would be confident of her husband's return, Jerry had no such assurance.

The boy's ulcer gradually improved as the relationship between the parents showed improvement, but twice during his early teens Jerry fell into situations in which he followed others who were poor examples. One evening he was playing with several other young teenagers when one suggested that they crawl in through the open window of a darkened house. Both boys entered and took several things, some of which proved to be quite valuable. The boys were later shamed by both the police and their own parents. However, some months later Jerry was again with a small group which included one boy who had recently run away from home and had returned with some drugs. Since there were too few drugs to go around, the boys raided medicine cabinets at home. They shook their collection of illicit drugs, aspirin, diet pills, birth control pills, etc., in a bowl and then each boy took a handful. The police found the boys in the early morning hours writhing on the ground near a warm air vent. Jerry suffered permanent heart damage as the effect of part of the drugs had been to speed his heart to an extremely strenuous rate. Perhaps if he had had a more approachable, interpersonally adequate father, one who would have guided him in the fashion indicated for the desirable personality characteristics discussed earlier in this chapter, Jerry could have been spared the ulcers, the low self-esteem which made him a follower, and perhaps other problems which still lie ahead of him as he matures.

Summary

There are a number of personality-social characteristics in children which are strongly influenced by particular behavior patterns of the parents, with the relationship influenced relatively little by the sex of either the parent or the child. Perhaps most characteristics could be expected to fall in this category rather than the category of behaviors closely related to sex-roles. In these behaviors the father's influence seems to be more or less identical with that of the mother. The research reviewed indicates that achievement motivation, aggression, and creativity in the child are among the behaviors which follow the example provided in the parents and reflect the encouragement of particular behaviors by the parents.

A cluster of very desirable and somewhat overlapping behaviors, including competence, high achievement motivation, self-esteem, successfulness internal-control, and, to a lesser estent, creativity, seem closely related to behavior patterns in the parents including high but reasonable expectations and demands of the child, consistent but rationally explained discipline, less punitive disciplinary techniques, clear and mutual communication with the child, and desirable models in the parents' own behavior.

Attitudes in such areas as politics, prejudice, and religion seem, especially in the younger child, to be imitated from those of the father and mother.

A number of psychological problems and disorders, initially viewed as a result of inadequacies in the mother's behavior, appear to be influenced at least as much by the father's behavior in those studies where investigators have made the effort to study the father's influence.

6 conclusions: increased effectiveness for fathers

Certain steps can be taken to place the information on the father's influence in perspective. One step is to take a look at the pattern of recent developments in certain other aspects of psychology.

One example comes from the research on the influences that determine parental behavior. At an earlier time a study would often focus on one single factor as a determinant of parental behavior toward children. Some studies looked at how the average parents from different levels of socioeconomic status favored different types of disciplinary practices. Other research focused on the number of parents at different levels of socioeconomic status who had used a particular source of information, such as government pamphlets. These studies did relatively little to explain the enormous variations in parent behavior that occur. Lois Stolz (1967) and her associates interviewed extensively thirty-nine pairs of parents concerning the influences on their behavior toward their children. As the investigators worked through the nearly nine thousand pages of transcripts typed from the recorded interviews, they sorted the comments of the parents into an average of 156 codings or units of information from each parent. As parents talked about why they behaved in particular ways with their children they were mentioning such influences as the importance of the child eating the right foods, beliefs about stages children pass through, the importance of the child obtaining a good education, the fact that the parent was irritable at a particular time, the setting in which an incident occurred, practices of the person's own parents, bad examples observed in other parents, influential experiences the person had had in his own childhood, advice from teachers, and a great many others. The results made it clear that there is unlikely to be one or even a few factors that are the causes of a parent's behavior with his children.

A similar pattern of development has occurred in research on drug use. At an earlier time the use of drugs was thought of by some as an "oral-dependent" behavior, and very likely the result of the infant's having been mishandled during the oral stage of development from birth to one year of age. A likely reason for a person to use drugs would be failure to breast feed or some inadequacy of the breast feeding the child received. Focus on such singular "causes" of drug related behavior was of little value. At a more recent point in the development of work on drug use, Jessor, Jessor, and Finney (1973) conducted a longitudinal study of marijuana use in over twelve hundred high school and university students. The authors obtained data on a broad range of influences on the individual's behavior. The personality characteristics studied included motivation for achievement and for independence, beliefs, and personal controls. The latter involved attitudes toward deviance and religiosity. Measured aspects of the individual's perceived social environment were parent-peer compatibility and social support for drug use. Specific aspects of the individual's behavior which were measured included beliefs about the effects of marijuana and behaviors of the individual that varied around usual adult moral standards. Taking into account this wide range of influences the authors were able to assign with 72.3 percent accuracy the fifty-three individuals out of 373 nonusers who had become users of marijuana by the subsequent school year.

This study and the study of influences on parental behavior can serve as examples of the greater effectiveness in understanding complex human behavior that results when investigators take into consideration multiple variables rather than searching for one cause. Generalizing from these examples to an understanding of the father's part in influencing the development of his children's behavioral characteristics, it seems obvious that the father's influence is some portion of an array of influences which include those from the mother, siblings, peers, the educational system, and the mass media, among many others.

Out of this array of influences it is difficult to determine the proportion due to the father. As can be seen in the preceding chapters, the most common tendency in statements about the father's influence is to underestimate it. The studies of absent or inadequate fathers show that even minimal behavior of the father is not completely lacking in influence, but instead is generally a negative one which helps to influence some of the children's characteristics away from the norm in an undesirable direction. Yet statements suggesting that the father has very little or no influence are numerous, while overestimates are rare.

Among the influences on children in a typical family, it seems quite likely that the parents provide the greatest single influence on children until some point during the adolescent years. The general pattern of research results on personality-social development suggests this, although little of it has been intended to determine the relative contribution of the various sources of influence. Influences from teachers, peers, and the mass media tend to be temporary and variable. While the child usually lives with the same set of parents for nearly two decades, the teacher along with the teacher's characteristics and opinions is different each school year.

The child's peers change very rapidly in the early years. In later years the influence of peers usually seems to be confined to particular situations rather than a determinant of consistent characteristics of the child, although research on this question is minimal. The case of Jerry (Chapter 5) seems typical of the kind of peer influences that are of concern to adults. In the incidents Jerry became involved in, groups of peers suggested the illegal activities and Jerry went along with them. But it seems likely that the personality deficiencies which led him to choose these friends and to to along with their risky suggestions resulted largely from the inadequacies of his parents' influence.

The mass media also tend to be temporary and situational in influence. It may be that such pervasive themes as the use of sex to sell products or magazines may help to shape attitudes toward sex. But more generally the content of magazines and the themes of television programs and movies seem to shift frequently.

Siblings share with parents a long, regular association with the child, but they typically do not share with parents either the strength of influence that comes from the rewarding or punishing behavior of the parent, or the potential model for observational learning that the parents provide. There is evidence, however, that older siblings have an increased potential for serving as models to younger children (Rosenberg & Sutton-Smith, 1970).

A second consideration about the proportion of influence that comes from parents is their control over other influences in the array. While some parents leave much of their potential control to chance through taking a *laissez-faire* approach to child-rearing, the typical parent can and does exert varying amounts of direct or indirect control on the other influences on his child. The child's siblings are obviously under the influence of the parents and generally similar to them in their characteristics. Much of a parent's interaction with his children is spent in dealing with the interactions between siblings, and in this way the parent is modifying the influence of one of his children upon the other.

It is difficult for a particular parent to exert much control over his child's school or his teacher. But parents often do inquire about the school system before moving to a new area, send their children to private or parochial schools, or have their child transferred from a particular teacher's classroom. Less directly, the parents' attitudes and values concerning education, homework, and so on mediate the child's reaction to his education. In the writer's work with one family, all four of the children, though they were near average in intelligence, were doing poorly in school and their dislike of reading seemed to be a key factor. This seemed to be closely linked to the parents' attitudes and example, as both of them were high school dropouts who rarely read anything, but did watch television steadily.

As the last example illustrates, the parents can control what mass media influences are allowed into the home. The writer and his wife, after consulting with the children to determine which television programs are their favorites, ban television watching on other week nights and restrict the watching time to one hour on the favored nights. The family has subscribed to several magazines of interest to the children, and books are typically included among gifts given to the children. At present there are very few movies that are judged to be suitable for watching as a family. However, the consensus of the research on the effects of television on children seems to be that such television themes as aggression mainly affect children who are already aggressive, and that with normal children the values and attitudes within the family can predominate over those observed on television.

There is a fair amount of evidence that the peers of the same or opposite sex that the child chooses as friends tend to be consistent with the socioeconomic status and other characteristics of his parents. Thus, their influence may be largely compatible with that of the parents. There is evidence that there is room for parental concern about the weight of peer influence in North America. Bronfenbrenner and his associates (1967b) presented twelve-year-olds in Russia and the United States with situations involving a choice between an antisocial behavior urged by peers and a moral behavior that adults would support, and the twelve-year-olds were asked to indicate which they would really choose. A typical situation involves the child finding a paper lost by the teacher with the questions and answers to tomorrow's quiz. The child is asked how likely he would be to go along with his classmates who urge that they all share the information and not say anything to the teacher. The Russian children responded strongly in the adult-desired direction, whether they were told that peers or adults would see their answers. The American children appeared to be almost as much influenced by the antisocial, peer-oriented choices as by the adult-favored choices. It is possible of course that the American children were less afraid to answer frankly than the Russian children.

A second illustration of heavy peer influence on a particular behavior comes from the numerous studies aimed at determining the factors which lead children in junior high and high school to begin to smoke. Influence from the parents is often indicated. In studying ninth graders Williams (1973) found that 23.5 percent of the boys smoked if the father did, as compared to 15 percent if he did not, while the same figures related to the mother's smoking were 21 and 17.3 percent. The girls seemed more influenced by parents, since 52 percent of them smoked if the father did and only 25 percent if he did not, while the same figures for the mother were 60 and 24.6 percent. However, about 80 to 90 percent of the junior and senior high school students whose friends smoke are smokers themselves, while about 10 to 20 percent of the junior high nonsmokers and 50 to 60 percent of the senior high nonsmokers have friends who smoke (Levitt and Edwards, 1970; Salber, Reed, Harrison, and Grien, 1963). Levitt and Edwards found that the smoking behavior of friends accounted for over 36 percent of the variation in the students' smoking behavior as compared to a minimal degree of variation accounted for by parental smoking behavior.

Again, however, the degree of influence that peers can have on the child may depend on the previous behavior of the parents. Bronfenbrenner (1970) studied peer-oriented and adult-oriented sixth-graders. He concluded that the peer-oriented children were influenced more by the lack of attention and concern at home than by the attractiveness of the peer group. Their parents were rated lower than the others on providing affection, support, discipline, and control. Bronfenbrenner suggests that the peer-oriented youngsters turned to the peer group to fill something of a vacuum resulting from the decreased parenting behavior often characteristic of today's urban families in North America. His findings suggest that parents who are actively and effectively involved in guiding their children are less likely to find their influence overruled by the children's peers.

From this it can be seen that the parents' influence on the child extends well beyond that which occurs in their direct interaction with the child. While it is probably not possible to indicate quantitatively what proportion of the total influence on the child comes from his parents, and while the degree of parental influence varies in different families, it does seem clear that the greatest single influence on the development of personality-social characteristics of children comes from the parents.

In focusing on the father's influence then, an additional question concerns the relative influence of the father as compared to the mother. A consideration of the two parents as if they were two completely separate sources of influence is probably artificial, since, as Stolz (1967) found, a typical parent seems to react to children with a blend of his own inclinations and consideration of the views of his spouse. In many instances a child may receive a response from one parent that includes implicitly the influence of the other, a joint response from both parents in the same discussion, or the answer, "It's all right with me if it's all right with your mother (father)." With this conjoint influence recognized, it is also true that each parent provides an independent influence on the child at times. This would occur when the behavior involved is of interest to only one of the parents. A teenage daughter interested in medicine might confer about her career plans with her veterinarian father rather than her mother who is a mechanical drawing teacher. Many examples of singular influence would involve sex role differences that differentiate between the activities of a child of one sex and his or her parent's activities. In some families, probably disturbed ones, each parent acts independently of the other or even in competition with the other in dealing with the child.

There are a number of recent studies which compare the relative influence of mothers and fathers in limited situations. In the study by Hetherington and Frankie (1967) described in Chapter 3, children could imitate the behavior of either the mother or the father. In the majority of comparisons studied these four- to six-year-olds imitated the mother more. However, in the families in which the father was dominant, the boys were more likely to imitate the father, and this tended to be true for the girls as well if there was a high level of conflict between the parents along with the father's dominance.

In a second example eleven- or sixteen-year-old sons and their parents made choices independently, and then the three were brought together to discuss the choices and arrive at a single family view (Jacob, 1974). During the discussion the interruptions, talking time, and degree of compromise were determined for each of these three members of the family. From the compromise data in particular it was clear that the father was the most influential person in the discussions, except in the case of a lower class family with a sixteen-year-old son. The authors noted that with a preadolescent son the pattern of influence tended to be father equal to mother, with mother more influential than the son. With an adolescent son, the mother and the son were similar in influence and second to the father in the middle class families, while there was near equality in influence among the three members of lower class families.

The demonstration of relative influence in these experimental situations is a different thing from the presently impossible task of assessing the relative contribution of each parent in influencing the personality-social development of the child. However, they do serve to illustrate that the influence of each parent varies with the situation, age and sex of the child, etc. They also demonstrate that the father's influence is not only more than negligible, it exceeds that of the mother at times. In comparing parents in their influences on children there seems to be little reason to challenge the impression dominant in our culture that the mother is the parent with the most influence on children. However, for particular areas of behavior, perhaps sex-role learning, development of quantitative skills, choosing an occupation, and others, the father's influence may typically exceed that of the mother for children of either sex. In most families the father's influence on the male child may be greater than that of the mother. One might consider here as well the fact that there are an estimated 660,000 families in the United States and Canada in which the *only* parent present in the home is the father. For a general picture, however, it is probably more appropriate to view the parents as having a combined influence rather than an autonomous one.

A couple of other points deserve emphasis, as they seem to be considered so seldom. One is that with the exception of behaviors linked to sex roles, the particular behaviors of the parents that have been shown to be related to motives, attitudes, and other behaviors of the child can apparently be performed as well by either parent. Similarly many of the effects of father absence may illustrate primarily that, because of the checks and balances which result, two parents are better than one. With the exception of behaviors linked to sex-role in our culture, it may well be completely a myth that there is anything unique about the influence of either parent that would prevent the father from having an influence on children equal to that of the mother. This may well be called for if present trends in changing sex-roles for women continue. A second point worth emphasizing is that, although it seems likely that at present the typical father has less influence on his children than the mother does, this does not mean, as writers often assume, that his influence is not substantial.

Fathers and the present effectiveness of socialization

Thinking about fathers and their influence as parents gains in significance with consideration of the degree of effectiveness with which we now prepare children to become successful adults. As a discussion question this writer has sometimes asked groups of university students to consider the people they know and indicate what proportion of them seem to have significant handicaps of a personality-social nature in pursuing their ordinary occupational and personal goals. Although university students probably are acquainted with a somewhat privileged rather than completely typical group of people, they generally indicate that about 50 percent of the people they know have problems that seriously hinder their functioning in the normal activities of an adult.

Recent years have been marked by widespread public concern about racism, war, and the wasteful destruction of the environment. A major problem that has yet to receive this kind of attention is the ineffectiveness of socialization, or, to put it another way, our destruction of people. There are a great many statistics one can point to that support the impression of the university students. There is the figure of one person in ten spending part of his life in a mental hospital. The figure for people being sent to jails and penitentiaries is similar. Among young people meeting the adjustment demands of adulthood, suicide is a leading cause of death. For just one bridge, the Golden Gate Bridge in San Francisco, the number of "successfully" completed suicide attempts is about five-hundred, and that does not include those stopped by personnel on the bridge. One out of two cases in the United States and one out of three in Canada of one person trying to live successfully in marriage with a favorite person ends in divorce. Physicians indicate that two-thirds of the people coming to see them do so because of personal or emotional problems rather than a problem needing strictly medical care. People fired from their jobs are apparently fired more often because of inability to get along with other people than because of inability to perform the other aspects of the position. One can also count millions of alcoholics, drug addicts, and many others among society's failures.

It is probably not possible to add such figures together and obtain an overall percentage of "unsatisfactory" results of socialization. Some unfortunate individuals turn up in several of these statistics when they should only be counted once. Some of these cases result from factors other than the inadequacy of the personality-social development of the individual. However, whether we are talking about 25 percent or 50 percent of the population, the point is that many millions of people live unsatisfactory lives, often bringing misery to their relatives or victims as well.

The ineffective behaviors of these people are primarily behaviors that are learned during childhood. The research reviewed in this book is only a small part of the total evidence for this statement. The source of influence that is most consistently in a favorable position to influence the child during his socialization is the parents. Thus, if we are to begin to deal with these massive problems through efforts to prepare children more effectively to deal with the life that will challenge them as they near and enter adulthood, it is important to recognize that one of the major sources of influence in the child's socialization is that "other" parent that is so often overlooked.

Some psychologists have begun to make specific proposals concerning the problem of inadequacy in some parents and its results (Lifur, 1973; McIntire, 1973). They notice the shocking headlines in almost every copy of urban newspapers that tell of yet another tragic incident committed by a disturbed person raised by inadequate parents. They see the misery that is behind the evidence of inadequate socialization cited above, figures that do not usually shock because we have somehow come to accept them as if we could do no better. They consider the urgent necessity for limiting the unlimited right of people to produce children as the world becomes increasingly overpopulated and as famine has already begun to cause thousands of deaths. They consider also the flood of useful information concerning adequate socialization of children by parents that has become available within the last decade or so through research in the social sciences. They conclude that we now know a great deal about how to do well at socializing children, but the whole process still contains great elements of chance in the socializing of most children. Dr. Roger McIntire, a University of Maryland psychology professor, comments in a *Psychology Today* article:

> In the case of child abusing parents, the state attempts to prevent the most obvious physical mistreatment of children. But our culture makes almost no demands when it comes to the children's psychological well-being and development. Any fool can now raise a child any way he or she pleases, and it's none of our business. The child becomes the unprotected victim of whoever gives birth to him. (p. 36)

> Can you imagine the public outcry that would occur if adoption agencies offered their children on a first-come-first-served basis, with no screening process for applicants? Imagine some drunk stumbling up and saying, "I'll take that cute little blond-haired girl over there." (p. 143)

> It seems that our society cares more about the selection of a child's second set of parents than it does about his original parents. (p. 36)

These authors suggest that as contraception technology progresses to make it possible, and as people come to say, "If your child is to live with us, be educated by us, suffered by us, add to the crowd of us, we should have a say," it may become the practice to screen potential parents. Some with inadequate child-rearing knowledge, emotional instability, genetic defects, or lack of intellectual competence would not be permitted to have children unless or until their significant problems could be corrected.

Such an idea is highly controversial of course and

many people have strong critical reactions to it. However, at a discussion of this possibility led by Linda Lifur (1973), Assemblyman Willie Brown of the California legislature participated in the discussion. He indicated, of course, that something like licensing of parents was not something voters would accept in the immediate future. However, California has a massive population squeezed into three metropolitan areas. Its people have been shocked repeatedly by bizarre mass murders, kidnappings, assassination, drugged youth cults, etc. In reaction to these influences and the massive tax burden of billions of dollars per year spent in dealing with these socialization failures, the state's voters have been pushing the politicians to examine and correct the defects in the process of socializing children to be an effective part of society. Assemblyman Brown indicated that the first steps taken may be those of making counseling available to people who decide to have children and providing something like tax incentives to encourage potential parents to make use of this voluntary counseling. Such intervention would be mild compared to the possibility of compulsory licensing for parents.

Less controversial methods of trying to lessen the failure rate in rearing members of our society include educational approaches such as increasing the number of secondary schools that offer, as some do already, courses in psychology or family relations. Such courses, and the discussion and experience dealing with children sometimes involved in them, may close part of the gap between potential and actual socialization of children, especially if they are required of females *and* males. An alternative approach might be to have a professional person visit each child at periodic intervals, perhaps when he was three and again when he was eight. At such visits the professional, or team of professionals, could examine the child sufficiently to detect any alarming problems in physical and psychological development. Remedies for any severe problems could then be arranged with the cooperation of the parents, or, in the small proportion of cases in which the parents were incompetent or uncooperative, without their cooperation. This kind of procedure is in operation now in most areas of North America, but in an informal and haphazard way. A neighbor, teacher, or other person who notices severe physical or psychological problems of a child that are not being dealt with by the parents can bring about intervention by child welfare or law enforcement officials. Yet the present system often fails to work because people fail to recognize severe problems in children, or choose not to get involved even if they do see the problems.

One of many indications of the need for a greater focus on child-rearing within the school system comes from research on child abuse involving physical injury (Spinetta and Rigler, 1972). Some authors have attempted to attribute the problem of child abuse to the low socioeconomic status of the parents, or to a psychotic condition in the abusing parent. However, these are not adequate explanations of the causation of abuse, since many of the parents involved are from middle or upper levels of socioeconomic status and few are severely psychotic. Several authors point to ignorance about child-rearing and inappropriate expectations for the child as common to abusing parents.

> The authors seem to agree that abusing parents lack appropriate knowledge of child-rearing, and that their attitudes, expectations, and child-rearing techniques set them apart from nonabusive parents. The abusing

parents implement culturally accepted norms for raising children with an exaggerated intensity and at an
inappropriately early age. (Spinetta and Rigler, 1972,
p. 299)

Considering our society's almost complete lack of
preparation of men for their role as fathers it is not
surprising that men are overrepresented among child-
abusing parents. One group of child-abusing parents is
made up of men who, because of some disability, are
unable to support their families, and are at home caring
for the children while the mothers work. Providing
future parents with the knowledge that would enable
them to form more reasonable expectations of their
children and more appropriate child-rearing techniques
would of course be only part of a solution to the child-
abuse problem, as it is very frequently the case that the
abusing parent suffered abuse or severe neglect himself as
a child. As Spinetta and Rigler observe, "The capacity to
love is not inherent; it must be taught to the child." This
aspect of the abusive parent problem probably requires
intervention in addition to increased course offerings on
child rearing.

Whether such organized efforts to improve parental
influence on their children's personality-social development gain acceptance, or whether we are left with the
improbable hope that ineffective parents will become less
frequent in future generations, it would help if the
present unrealistic view of the father's influence held by
many could be corrected. It appears to this writer that the
average father is actually, or certainly potentially, the
second greatest influence in his children's development,
and this influence is likely to be used ineffectively if both
he and the child's mother, teacher, and others are
unaware of it.

Characteristics of ideal fathers

Many men have been outstanding fathers, and most of them have probably accomplished this without being particularly self-conscious about their role. On the other hand a question that has apparently not been researched is, what proportion of fathers have unnecessarily spent extra time away from their children in work or recreation, have left the guidance of the children to a mother with limited effectiveness, or have been capricious in interactions with their children because they viewed their role as an inconsequential one as it is often pictured? It seems likely that the functioning of male parents would be greatly improved if they were more uniformly aware that their actions, even the "nonactions" just listed, are helping to shape the characteristics of their children. All fathers need to be disabused of the myths that because they have a forty-hour-a-week job they can have no impact on their children, that males can have little influence on children because they lack the "maternal instincts" of the female, or that fathers "lost their effectiveness" with the transition away from the traditional family of former years. For these and related reasons a desirable characteristic of fathers would be an awareness of the range and degree of their influence as that is shown in the research reviewed in preceding chapters.

An obvious correlate of fathers being aware of their influence is their presence and involvement with their children to a sufficient degree to exercise a positive influence. Identification is described as following from a situation in which the "child becomes dependent on a continued flow of affection and in which a continued supply of affection is contingent on conformity to demands," and we have seen that this kind of relationship between the father and either his son or daughter is related to better general adjustment. Relatively close involvement of the father with his children is also linked to higher creativity, and, in sons, to nondelinquency.

How much time it takes to make enough "presence" isn't clear. There are several indications that consistent absence of the father for weeks or months leads to destructive effects, yet some of the findings concerning working mothers indicate that relatively small numbers of hours regularly set aside to spend with the children appeared sufficient to cancel out any negative effects due to the mother's absence for work.

Some laymen and professionals hold a unique view of the role which parents should play in assisting the development of personality-social characteristics in their children. The view is one of self-actualization or it could be described as a "botanical theory." The belief is that the child has an innate force within him which will tend to lead him to develop desirable personality characteristics that are appropriate for him. This view suggests that the parents' part in this is to supply unconditional love and other caretaking, but otherwise leave the child to his own directions. Some examples of this view from interviews with parents by members of the writer's classes are:

(Father, forty-four years old) I would be more pleased to leave them and see in what direction they tend to go, rather than try to make them like what I like.

(Father, thirty-one years old, a truck driver) Trying to control a child and manipulate him according to your values was the worst thing parents could do in impairing a child's normal development.

Although the passive role that this view would suggest for fathers might sound appealing, there seems to be very little research evidence that this approach results in anything but undesirable characteristics in children. In contrast the research reviewed here has pointed consistently to desirable effects from a more active parental role, and the data, particularly in Chapter 5, is fairly consistent in supporting particular aspects of the role.

Control of the child, or establishment and enforcement of guidelines, seems to be a key issue. That seems to be synonymous with discipline, guidance or similar terms. It is clear that the ideal father should take an active role in establishing and consistently enforcing guidelines for the child. These guidelines for behavior should be fitted to the child so that they are somewhat challenging for his age and ability, but not excessively so. This points again to the need for a steady involvement with the child, as it is usually difficult for a person to know what levels of performance can be expected of a child without fairly continuous interaction with the child and close monitoring of the child's developing capability.

Obviously it is necessary for the parents to revise their guidelines with the age of the child. Revision would be necessary both when the child had progressed through experience and/or maturation so that higher standards could be expected of him, and when the child's progress makes it possible to drop external guidelines and turn more and more control over to him as he develops toward adult autonomy. Apparently the guidelines or rules should be broad and less numerous, so that many aspects of behavior can be left under the child's own control as soon as he is capable of autonomy in that area. For example the writer and his wife found that with each of their children supervision was necessary through the first few grades of school to see that the child completed homework projects on time. From parental help and the child's own experiences and motivation, a fifteen-year-old son is now obviously able to pace his homework entirely on his own, and is provided only the continued approval of his efforts by the parents. How the boy is doing would, of course, not be obvious if there were not regular talks between parents and children at the evening meal and at other times about how things are going at school.

Whatever the relationship between the husband and wife, it seems essential that the guidelines developed be pretty much mutually agreed upon. When each parent holds to a set of guidelines different than those of the spouse the effect on the child probably can't be anything like the desired consistency.

When the child's behavior does not meet reasonable expectations, there are advantages to using particular enforcement procedures, although it may be less important just how guidelines are enforced and most important that fathers do hold to them. While there seems to be little reason why physical punishment should be completely avoided, it has a number of disadvantages, including the risk, especially for fathers, of physical harm to the child, and the problem of setting a bad example for the child. The writer worked with one set of parents who illustrate the latter problem. They used a slap on the face to discipline their five children, the oldest two being over ten years of age. They had to discipline "about ninety-nine" times a day, a good indication of ineffectiveness, because the five children were forever slapping each other when they had conflicts. When the parents altered their disciplinary approach, and stopped hitting as a means of solving interpersonal disagreements, the slapping behavior of their children improved greatly.

One aspect of a more effective approach is that of

rewarding the child with privileges, praise, or in some other way when he behaves in a desirable manner rather than placing almost exclusive emphasis on punishment following poor behavior. We saw earlier that rewarding for successes was emphasized by the parents who had boys high in self-esteem, yet Stolz (1967), in her interview study of parents, found fathers to emphasize punishment for poor behavior five times as much as they emphasized reward for what the child did correctly. Mothers in the study were close behind with four times as much emphasis on punishing. This negative emphasis of parents seems ill-advised when the recent, extensive progress in "behavior modification" or operant conditioning with children has relied primarily and successfully on the use of positive reinforcement.

In addition to the emphasis on reward, the most effective parents in the studies cited have stressed discussion and reasoning with the child, and where punishment was used it was likely to be a technique such as denial of privileges or isolation of the child away from friends and family for a period of time.

Another characteristic of our ideal fathers that would fit with those above would be their pattern of communication with their children. The guidelines that are established for children need to be communicated to them clearly so that they can know what is expected of them. Additionally the most effective parents are receptive to the views of their children and encourage them to have a voice in the making of family plans, including some questioning of the decisions of the parents concerning the child.

The attitudes or emotions that should characterize fathers have not been as well clarified. Popular magazine articles on raising children often emphasize the general theme "give them lots of love and everything else will take care of itself." In contrast with that advice there seems to be little if any research showing that more affectionate parents have children who are happier or develop better in some way, except for the obvious fact that parents characterized as warm and approving are associated with optimal development, while unconcerned or hostile attitudes in the parents are frequently associated with serious problems in the children. Another aspect of parental attitudes that has often been shown to be related to their effectiveness is the area of expectations held by the parents concerning the child. Children who were more successful, high in achievement motivation, higher in self-esteem, and more believing in an internal locus of control had parents who communicated their high expectations to their children.

Probably the most frequent finding of a relationship between parental characteristics and the characteristics of their children relates a characteristic of the child to the occupational status of the father. The father's occupational status is a complex indicator of many characteristics of the family; for example fathers of higher occupational status would be more likely to be married to women with a higher than average education, and it could be that influence which was related to the child's having a particular, more desirable characteristic, such as an above-average interest in reading. However, in part of the research it is obvious that the effect of the father's occupational status on the child occurs more directly through the model that the father provides for the observational learning of the child. As would be predicted from the theories of observational learning discussed earlier, the child who sees in his father a person who is competent, respected by others or in authority over them, and/or who has been rather consistently successful, is more likely to imitate the behaviors of his or her father. This was most evident in the research showing the high rates with which male university students selected areas of study similar to their fathers' professions, but also in research on creativity, sexual orientation in females, and other areas.

It is also clear that the model the father provides of political views, religious beliefs, and attitudes toward people of varied ethnic characteristics or national origins helps to determine at least the initial and often the lifelong attitudes of his children on these topics. The same influence probably holds true on many other topics which have received less research attention, such as attitudes toward environmental issues, interest in sports, and, an area that has been researched, the decision whether or not to begin smoking cigarettes. It is not always possible to describe the example that would be provided by the ideal father, as one's attitudes on specific issues such as these are largely a matter of individual values. A father's intolerance of people on the basis of their ethnicity or national origin and positive attitudes toward smoking would be exceptions as there is little if anything that can be said in their defense.

People skeptical of psychology sometimes express the concern that widespread use of the findings of psychology in raising children would result in everyone being just alike, as if they were mass manufactured cookies. A careful look at the research relating parent behavior to optimal development of children shows that this is not the case. The characteristics of ideal fathers suggested above can be expected to help more of their children develop into people who generally do well at what they do, actively solve most of the problems they run into, feel positive about themselves, interact with other people effectively, and the like, but this does not involve any restriction in occupation, religious or political views, or any other desirable aspect of the multitude of possible life styles.

While a relationship has been found between each of these "ideal" parental behaviors and desirable characteristics in children, the opposite of each behavior has also been linked to undesirable characteristics in children.

Without his presence the research indicates that, either through the direct effects of the father not being present to perform his usual role with the children, or through the common indirect effects such as lowered socioeconomic status for the family and a greater burden on the mother, there is an increased risk of undesirable personality and social characteristics in the children. Detrimental effects of father absence have been shown in children's aggression, dependency, degree of adjustment or "psychopathology," delinquency rates, moral behavior, success in the Peace Corps or military service, premarital pregnancy rates, masculinity in males, and intellectual performance.

The failure of the father to establish and effectively enforce guidelines has been related in varying degrees to male homosexuality, delinquency, schizophrenia, low self-esteem, lower levels of competence and unsuccessfulness. Unreasonably low expectations of the child have been associated with lower self-esteem, less competence, and unsuccessfulness, while unreasonably high expectations are associated with aggressively high levels of assertiveness. Failure to enforce guidelines through the use of reward and punishment is typical of the parents of schizophrenics. Ineffective or minimal communication from the father has been shown to be common in the background of schizophrenics and male homosexuals. Rejection, hostile, or frightening behavior in the father has been linked to homosexuality in both males and females, as well as detrimental effects on cognitive performance in females, neurotic-inhibitory behavior, and antisocial behavior such as stealing and temper problems.

One obstacle to bringing fathers to a level of optimal knowledge, effectiveness, and involvement with their children may be the fathers' own perceptions of their role. Several authors have pointed to a built-in conflict in the socialization of males. Knox and Kupferer (1971) point out that male socialization still heavily emphasizes power, aggression, independence, achievement, and "competitive striving for success in the occupational world." This emphasis has its disadvantages "in short-comings in interpersonal competence and sensitivity," which is obviously prerequisite to effectiveness with children. There is some indication from one select sample (*Psychology Today* readers) that more of a family orientation in a man may not necessarily involve any sacrifice of progress in his career (Tavris, 1973). Family-oriented men, those who indicated it was their family which gave them the most satisfaction in life, were twice as likely to indicate they were very satisfied with their marriage as were career-oriented men. On the other hand the family-oriented men were almost as likely as the career-oriented men to say that they were working for the pleasure of it. The incomes of both groups were comparable, so there was no indication that less singleminded-ness about their career had caused any economic loss for the family-oriented men.

Benson (1968) has looked at the father's role from a sociological perspective. In his book he notes in part that the breadwinner aspect of the father's role has become of less significance as an increasing number of women are prepared for careers, and as governments offer more programs of assistance to families. Benson's prognosis is that the father will become more family oriented:

> In a sense the family has become more important to father, even as he has become relatively less important to the family. Once father was the prime agent of family strength; now he is often reliant upon it, especially for emotional sustenance. . . . A system seems to be emerging in which an important function of the family is to guarantee the highly skilled male a sense of interpersonal security. The family becomes the key to father's endurance as a skilled organism in the bureaucratic world. Impersonal forms of bureaucratic organization replace the kinship network as the strategic principle for work and social effort, and the small family becomes the man's emotional "home base" in the process. (p. 324)

In his book synthesizing his own and related research on the father's influence, Biller (1971b) notes that father-child involvement is not only of benefit to the child:

> The uninvolved father does not experience the gratification of actively facilitating the successful development of his children. He misses a meaningful opportunity to learn to deal in a sensitive way with many interpersonal situations. Widespread paternal inadequacy contributes to the existence of large numbers of interpersonally insensitive men. Many of these men are in positions of authority and their alienation as fathers has limited their ability to interact with young people. Inadequate paternal involvement is a factor in the problems of communication between individuals of different ages—contributing to the generation gap. (p. 128)

The increased involvement of the father in child

rearing, which would be desirable and which may be an increasing trend, does not primarily mean an increase in time spent in interaction with children. While such an increase may be crucial for some fathers who are deficient in that behavior, there is little evidence so far that the number of hours either parent spends with the children is closely related to the parents' effects on the children. Instead the main point is that fathers and those involved with fathers need to be more aware of the very significant influence of fathers on children, and aware of the pattern of fathering behavior which would result in the most desirable effects on the children's personality development.

Summary

Two points are particularly important in putting the father's influence on children in perspective. One is that a search for the one psychological variable that is responsible for some one behavior has seldom been fruitful. Recent research on several problems indicates that human behavior is more often influenced by an array of variables in both the person's past and in the particular present situation in which he behaves. The research indicates that the same holds true for the father's influence on the child's behavior. That is, it is seldom likely to be the only influence on either desirable or undesirable characteristics in the child, but rather is one part of an array of influences.

Nevertheless, a second point is that parents are in a unique position to be the most powerful single source of influence on a child, and the only consistent influence the child is exposed to throughout childhood. While the popular impression of the mother as more influential with children than the father is probably accurate for most families, the father remains actually or potentially the second greatest influence on the child, rather than the minor influence assumed in much contemporary literature.

As people look to the child-rearing situation for prevention of the human problems so widespread in our society, it is vital that the father's influence be viewed more realistically. The research available points strongly to a series of behaviors which, if practiced by fathers as well as mothers, seem likely to go far toward reducing our frequent ineffectiveness in the socialization of children.

bibliography

Aberle, D. F., and Naegele, K. D. Middle-class fathers' occupational role and attitudes toward children. *American Journal of Orthopsychiatry*, 1952, *22*, 366-78.

Anderson, R. E. Where's dad? Paternal deprivation and delinquency. *Archives of General Psychiatry*, 1968, *18*, 641-649.

Andry, R. G. Faulty paternal and maternal child-relationships, affection and delinquency. *British Journal of Delinquency*, 1960, *97*, 329-340.

———— Paternal and maternal roles and delinquency, deprivation of maternal care. Geneva, W.H.O. Public Health Papers No. 14, 1962, 31-44.

Another Nader, *Newsweek*, July 20, 1970.

Apperson, L. B., and McAdoo, W. G. Parental factors in the childhood of homosexuals. *Journal of Abnormal and Social Psychology*, 1968, *73*, 201-206.

Bach, G. R. Father-fantasies and father-typing in father separated children. *Child Development*, 1946, *17*, 63-80.

Bandura, A. *Aggression: A Social Learning Analysis.* Englewood Cliffs, N.J.: Prentice-Hall, 1973.

———— and Huston, Aeltha C. Identification as a

process of incidental learning. *Journal of Abnormal and Social Psychology*, 1961, *63*, 311-318.

_____ Ross, D., and Ross, S. A. Imitation of film-mediated aggressive models. *Journal of Abnormal and Social Psychology*, 1963, *66*, 3-11.

_____ and Walters, R. H. *Adolescent Aggression*. New York: Ronald Press, 1959.

_____ and Walters, R. H. *Social Learning and Personality Development*. New York: Holt, Rinehart & Winston, 1963.

Baraff, A. S., and Cunningham, A. P. Asthmatic and normal children. *Journal of The American Medical Association*, 1965, *192*, 99-101.

Barclay, A., and Cusumano, D. R. Father absence, cross-sex identity, and field dependent behavior in male adolescents. *Child Development*, 1967, *38*, 243-250.

Barglow, P., Bornstein, M., Exum, D. B., Wright, M. K., and Visotsky, H. M. Some psychiatric aspects of illegitimate pregnancy in early adolescence. *American Journal of Orthopsychiatry*, 1968, *38*, 672-687.

Barry, H., Bacon, M. K., and Child, I. L. A cross-cultural survey of some sex differences in socialization. *Journal of Abnormal and Social Psychology*, 1957, *55*, 327-332.

Bartemeier, L. The contribution of the father to the mental health of the family. *American Journal of Psychiatry*, 1953, *110*, 277-280.

Baruch, R. The achievement motive in women: Implications for career development. *Journal of Personality and Social Psychology*, 1967, *5*, 260-267.

Baumrind, D. Child care practices anteceding three patterns of preschool behavior. *Genetic Psychological Monographs*, 1967, *75*, 43-88.

_____ Socialization practices associated with

dimensions of competence in preschool boys and girls. *Child Development,* 1967, *38,* 291-327.

——————— Socialization and instrumental competence in young children. *Young Children,* 1970, *26,* 104-119.

Baxter, J. C., Horton, D. L., and Wiley, R. E. Father identification as a function of mother-father relationship. *Journal of Individual Psychology,* 1964, *20,* - 167-171.

Bell, A. P. Role modeling of fathers in adolescence and young adulthood. *Journal of Counseling Psychology,* 1969, *16,* 30-35.

Bene, E. On the genesis of male homosexuality: An attempt at clarifying the role of the parents. *British Journal of Psychiatry,* 1965, *111,* 803-813.

——————— On the genesis of female homosexuality. *British Journal of Psychiatry,* 1965, *111,* 815-821.

Benson, L. *Fatherhood: A Sociological Perspective.* New York: Random House, 1968.

Bieber, I., Dain, H. J., Dince, P. R., Drellich, M. G., Grand, H. G., Grundlach, R. H., Kremer, M. W., Rifkin, A. H., Wilbur, C. B., and Bieber, T. B. *Homosexuality: A Psychoanalytic Study.* New York: Basic Books, 1962.

Bieri, J. Parental identification, acceptance of authority, and within sex differences in cognitive behavior. *Journal of Abnormal and Social Psychology,* 1960, *60,* 76-79.

Biller, H. B. A note on father absence and masculine development in lower-class negro and white boys. *Child Development,* 1968, *39,* 1003-1006.

——————— Father dominance and sex-role development in kindergarten-age boys. *Developmental Psychology,* 1969, *1,* 87-94.

——————— Father absence, maternal encouragement, and

sex role development in kindergarten-age boys. *Child Development,* 1969, *40,* 539-546.

──────── Father absence and the personality development of the male child. *Developmental Psychology,* 1970, *2,* 181-201.

──────── The mother-child relationship and the father-absent boy's personality development. *Merrill-Palmer Quarterly,* 1971, *17,* 227-241 (a).

──────── *Father, Child, and Sex Role: Paternal determinants of personality development.* Lexington, Mass.: Heath Lexington Books, 1971 (b).

──────── and Bahm, R. M. Father absence, perceived maternal behavior, and masculinity of self-concept among junior high school boys. *Developmental Psychology,* 1970, *2,* 178-181.

──────── and Borstelmann, L. J. Masculine Development: An integrative review. *Merrill-Palmer Quarterly,* 1967, *13,* 253-294.

──────── and Weiss, S. D. The father-daughter relationship and the personality development of the female. *Journal of Genetic Psychology,* 1970, *116,* 79-93.

Bishop, D. W., and Chace, C. A. Parental conceptual systems, home play environment, and potential creativity in children. *Journal of Experimental Child Psychology,* 1971, *12,* 318-338.

Block, J., Jennings, P. H., Harvey, E., and Simpson, E. Interaction between allergic potential and psychopathology in childhood asthma. *Psychosomatic Medicine,* 1964, *26,* 307-320.

Blum, S. What makes a good father. *Redbook,* 1964, 122 (JA), 38-94.

Bowlby, J. *Maternal Care and Mental Health.* Geneva: World Health Organization, 1952.

Bradburn, N. M. Achievement and father dominance in Turkey. *Journal of Abnormal and Social Psychology*, 1963, *67*, 464-468.

Brim, O. G. Family structure and sex role learning by children: A further analysis of Helen Koch's data. *Sociometry*, 1958, *21*, 1-16.

Bronfenbrenner, U. The psychological costs of quality and equality in education. *Child Development*, 1967, *38*, 909-925 (a).

_____ Response to pressure from peers versus adults among Soviet and American school children. *International Journal of Psychology*, 1967, *2*, 199-207 (b).

_____ *Two worlds of childhood: U.S. and U.S.S.R.* New York: Russell Sage Foundation, 1970.

Brown, D. G. Sex-role preferences in young children. *Psychological Monographs*, 1956, No. 14 (Whole No. 421).

_____ The development of sex-role inversion and homosexuality. *Journal of Pediatrics*, 1957, *50*, 613-619.

_____ Inversion and homosexuality. *American Journal of Orthopsychiatry*, 1958, *28*, 424-429.

_____ The psychology of fatherhood. *Vital Speeches*, 1961, *27*, 700-704.

Bullock, A. *Hitler: A Study in Tyranny*. London:Odhams Books, 1964.

Burton, R. V., and Whiting, J. W. M. The absent father and cross-sex identity. *Merrill-Palmer Quarterly*, 1961, *7*, 85-95.

Byrne, D. Parental antecedents of authoritarianism. *Journal of Personality and Social Psychology*, 1965, *1*, 369-373.

_____ *An Introduction To Personality: Research, Theory, and Applications*. New Jersey: Prentice-Hall, Inc., 1974.

Carlsmith, L. Effect of early father absence on scholastic aptitude. *Harvard Educational Review*, 1964, *34*, 3-21.

Carter, V. B. *Winston Churchill as I Knew Him*. London: Eyre and Spothiswoode and Collins, 1965.

Cavallin, H. Incestuous fathers: A clinical report. *American Journal of Psychiatry*, 1966, *122*, 1132-1138.

Cheek, F. E. The father of the schizophrenic: The function of a peripheral role. *Archives of General Psychiatry*, 1965, *13*, 336-345.

Cohen, M. S. A man is daddy. *Redbook*, 1965, *125* (JE), 60+.

Colfax, J. D., and Allen, I. L. Pre-coded versus open-ended items and children's reports of father's occupation. *Sociology of Education*, 1967, *40*, 96-98.

Connell, D. M., and Johnson, J. E. The relationship between sex-role identification and self-esteem in early adolescents. *Developmental Psychology*, 1970, *3*, 268.

Coopermsith, S. *The antecedents of self-esteem*. San Francisco: W. H. Freeman & Co., 1967.

Cox, F. N. An assessment of the achievement behavior system in children. *Child Development*, 1962, *33*, 907-916.

Crain, A. J., and Stamm, C. S. Intermittent absence of fathers and children's perception of parents. *Journal of Marriage and The Family*, 1965, *27*, 344-347.

Crandall, V. C. *Differences in parental antecedents of internal-external Control in Children and in Young Adulthood*. Paper presented at the meeting of the American Psychological Association, Montreal, August, 1973.

Crites, J. O. Parental identification in relation to vocational interest development. *Journal of Educational Psychology,* 1962, *53,* 262-270.

Da Silva, G. The role of the father with chronic schizophrenic patients. *Canadian Psychiatric Association Journal,* 1963, *8,* 190-203.

Davidson, P. O., and Schrag, A. R. The role of the father in guidance clinic consultations. *Journal of Psychology,* 1968, *68,* 249-256.

Dellas, M., and Gaier, E. L. Identification of creativity: The individual. *Psychological Bulletin,* 1970, *73,* 55-73.

Deutsch, H. *The Psychology of Women.* Vol. I. New York: Grune and Stratton, 1944.

Deutsch, M. Minority group and class status as related to social and personality factors in scholastic achievement. *Society of Applied Anthropology Monographs,* 1960, No. 2.

——— and Brown B. Social influences in Negro-white intelligence differences. *Journal of Social Issues,* 1964, *20,* 24-35.

Deutscher, M. Adult work and developmental models. *American Journal of Orthopsychiatry,* 1968, *38,* 882-892.

Dorpat, T. L., Jackson, J. K., and Ripley, H. S. Broken homes and attempted and completed suicide. *Archives of General Psychiatry,* 1965, *12,* 213-216.

Droppleman, L. F., and Schaefer, E. S. Boy's and girl's reports of maternal and paternal behavior. *Journal of Abnormal and Social Psychology,* 1963, *67,* 648-654.

Eisenberg, L. The fathers of autistic children. *American Journal of Orthopsychiatry,* 1957, *27,* 715-725.

Elkind, D. The ,child's conception of his religious

denomination I: The Jewish Child. *Journal of Genetic Psychology*, 1961, *99*, 209-225.

_____ The child's conception of his religious denomination II: The Catholic Child. *Journal of Genetic Psychology*, 1962, *101*, 185-193.

_____ The child's conception of his religious denomination III: The Protestant Child. *Journal of Genetic Psychology*, 1963, *103*, 291-304.

Ellison, E. A., and Hamilton, D. M. The hospital treatment of dementia praecox: Part II. *American Journal of Psychiatry*, 1949, *106*, 454-461.

Epstein, R., and Komorita, S. S. Childhood prejudice as a function of parental ethnocentrism, punitiveness and outgroup characteristics. *Journal of Personality and Social Psychology*, 1966, *3*, 259-264 (a).

_____ and Komorita, S. S. Prejudice among Negro children as related to parental ethnocentrism and punitiveness. *Journal of Personality and Social Psychology*, 1966, *4*, 643-647 (b).

Eron, L. D., Banta, T. J., Walder, L. O., and Laulicht, J. H. Comparison of data obtained from mothers and fathers on child rearing practices and their relation to child aggression. *Child Development*, 1961, *32*, 457-472.

Evans, R. B. Childhood parental relationships of homosexual men. *Journal of Consulting and Clinical Psychology*, 1969, *33*, 129-135.

Flacks, R. The liberated generation: An exploration of the roots of student protest. *Journal of Social Issues*, 1967, *3*, 52-75.

Forrest, T. Paternal roots of female character development. *Contemporary Psychoanalysis*, 1966, *3*, 21-38.

———— The paternal roots of female character development. *Psychoanalytic Review,* 1967, *54,* 81-99.

Gardner, L. P. A survey of the attitudes and activities of fathers. *Journal of Genetic Psychology,* 1943, *63,* 15-53.
———— Analysis of children's attitudes to fathers. *Journal of Genetic Psychology,* 1947, *70,* 3-38.

Gardner, R. C., Taylor, D. M., and Feenstra, H. J. Ethnic stereotypes: Attitudes or beliefs. *Canadian Journal of Psychology,* 1970, *24,* 321-334.

Gerard, D. L., and Siegel, J. The family background of schizophrenia. *Psychiatric Quarterly,* 1950, *24,* 47-73.

Ginandes, S. One man no woman ever escapes. *Redbook,* 1971, *136* (Apr.), 73+.

Glaser, E. M., & Ross, H. L. *A Study of Successful Persons from Seriously Disadvantaged Backgrounds.* Washington, D. C.: Department of Labor, Office of Special Manpower Programs, March, 1970.

Glueck, S., and Glueck, E. *Delinquents and Nondelinquents in Perspective.* Cambridge, Mass.: Harvard University Press, 1968.

Goodenough, E. W. Interest in persons as an aspect of sex differences in the early years. *Genetic Psychology Monographs,* 1957, *55,* 287-323.

Gorer, G. *The American People: A study of national character.* New York: Norton, 1948.

Gosse, E. *Father and Son: Biographical Recollections.* New York: Charles Scribner's, 1907.

Gray, S. W. Perceived similarity to parents and adjustment. *Child Development,* 1959, *30,* 91-107.

Green, M. R. (Ed.). *Interpersonal psychoanalysis: The*

selected papers of Clara M. Thompson. New York: Basic Books, 1964.

Greenstein, F. I. *Children and Politics.* New Haven: Yale University Press, 1965.

Greenstein, J. M. Father characteristics and sex typing. *Journal of Personality and Social Psychology,* 1966, *3,* 271-277.

Gregory, I. Anterospective data following childhood loss of a parent, II. Pathology, performance and potential among college students. *Archives of General Psychiatry,* 1965, *13,* 2, 110-120.

Gronseth, E., and Tiller, P. O. The impact of father-absence in sailor families upon the personality structure and social adjustment of adult sailor sons. Part I. In Anderson (Ed.), *Studies of the Family,* Vol. 2, Gottingen: Vandenhoeck and Ruprecht, 1957, 97-114.

Gundlach, R. H. Childhood parental relationships and the establishment of gender roles of homosexuals. *Journal of Consulting and Clinical Psychology,* 1969, *33,* 136-139.

Hall, C. S., and Lindzey, G. *Theories of Personality.* New York: Wiley & Sons, 1957.

Hampson, J. L. Determinants of psychosexual orientation. In F. A. Beach (Ed.), *Sex and Behavior.* New York: Wiley, 1965.

Heiden, K. *Der Fuehrer: Hitler's Rise to Power.* Boston: Houghton Mifflin, 1944.

Heilbrun, A. B. Parental model attributes, nurturant reinforcement, and consistency of behavior in adolescents. *Child Development,* 1964, *35,* 151-167.

————— Social value: Social behavior consistency, parental identification and aggression in late adolescence. *Journal of Genetic Psychology*, 1964, *104*, 135-146.

_____ Sex differences in identification learning. *Journal of Genetic Psychology*, 1965, *106*, 185-193.

_____ An empirical test of the modeling theory of sex role learning. *Child Development*, 1965, *36*, 789-799.

_____ Sex role, instrumental-expressive behavior, and psychopathology in females. *Journal of Abnormal Psychology*, 1968, *73*, 2, 131-136.

_____ Sex-role identity in adolescent females: A theoretical paradox. *Adolescence*, 1968, *3*, 79-88.

_____ Parental identification and the patterning of vocational interests in college males and females. *Journal of Counseling Psychology*, 1969, *16*, 342-347.

_____ and Fromme, D. K. Parental identification of late adolescents and level of adjustment: The importance of parent-model attributes, ordinal position, and sex of child. *Journal of Genetic Psychology*, 1965, *107*, 49-59.

_____ Harrell, S. N., and Gillard, B. J. Perceived childrearing attitudes of fathers and cognitive controls in daughters. *Journal of Genetic Psychology*, 1967, *111*, 29-40.

_____ Orr, H. K., and Harrell, S. N. Patterns of parental childrearing and subsequent vulnerability to cognitive disturbance. *Journal of Consulting Psychology*, 1966, *30*, 51-59.

Helper, M. M. Learning theory and the self concept. *Journal of Abnormal and Social Psychology*, 1955, *51*, 184-194.

Helson, R. Personality characteristics and developmental history of creative college women. *Genetic Psychology Monographs*, 1967, *76*, 205-256.

_____ Effects of sibling characteristics and parental

values on creative interest and achievement. *Journal of Personality,* 1968, *36,* 589-607.

———— and Crutchfield, R. S. Creative types in mathematics. *Journal of Personality,* 1970, *38,* 177-197.

Herzog, E., and Sudia, C. E. Fatherless homes: A review of research. *Children,* 1968, *15,* 177-182.

———— and Sudia, C. E. *Boys In Fatherless Families.* Washington, D.C.: Dept. of Health, Education, and Welfare, 1970.

Hetherington, E. M. A developmental study of the effects of sex of the dominant parent on sex-role preference, identification, and imitation in children. *Journal of Personality and Social Psychology,* 1965, *2,* 188-194.

———— Effects of paternal absence on sex-typed behaviors in Negro and white preadolescent males. *Journal of Personality and Social Psychology,* 1966, *4,* 87-91.

———— Girls without fathers. *Psychology Today,* 1973, *6,* 47-52.

———— and Frankie, G. Effects of parental dominance, warmth, and conflict on imitation in children. *Journal of Personality and Social Psychology,* 1967, *6,* 119-125.

Hjelholt, G. The neglected parent. *Acta Psychologica,* 1958, *10,* 179-184.

Hoffman, M. L. Father absence and conscience development. *Developmental Psychology,* 1971, *4,* 400-406.

Hooker, E. Parental relations and male homosexuality in patient and nonpatient samples. *Journal of Consulting and Clinical Psychology,* 1969, *33,* 140-142.

Illsley, R., and Thompson, B. Women from broken homes. *Sociological Review,* 1961, *9,* 27-54.

Jacob, T. Patterns of Family conflict and dominance as a

function of child age and social class. *Developmental Psychology*, 1974, *10*, 1-12.

Jacobson, G., and Ryder, R. G. Parental loss and some characteristics of the early marriage relationship. *American Journal of Orthopsychiatry*, 1969, *39*, 779-787.

Jessor, R., Jessor, S. L., and Finney, J. A social psychology of marijuana use: Longitudinal studies of high school and college youth. *Journal of Personality and Social Psychology*, 1973, *26*, 1-15.

Johnson, M. M. Sex-role learning in the nuclear family. *Child Development*, 1963, *34*, 319-333.

Josselyn, Irene M. Cultural forces, motherliness and fatherliness. *American Journal of Orthopsychiatry*, 1956, *26*, 264-271.

Kagan, J. The child's perception of the parent. *Journal of Abnormal and Social Psychology*, 1956, *53*, 257-258.

————— Hosken, B., and Watson, S. Child's symbolic conceptualization of parents. *Child Development*, 1961, *32*, 625-636.

Kanner, L., and Eisenberg, L. Notes on the follow-up studies of autistic children. In P. H. Hoch and J. Zubin (Eds.), *Psychopathology of Childhood*, New York: Grune & Stratton, 1955, pp. 227-234.

Kaye, H. E., et al. Homosexuality in women. *Archives of General Psychiatry*, 1967, *17*, 626-634.

Kayton, R., and Biller, H. B. Perception of parental sex-role behavior and psychopathology in adult males. *Journal of Consulting and Clinical Psychology*, 1970, *36*, 235-237.

Kirby, D. M., and Gardner, R. C. Ethnic stereotypes: Norms on 208 words typically used in their assessment. *Canadian Journal of Psychology*, 1972, *26*, 140-154.

Knox, W. E., and Kupferer, H. J. A discontinuity in the

socialization of males in the United States. *Merrill-Palmer Quarterly*, 1971, *17*, 251-261.

Kohlberg, L. A cognitive-developmental analysis of children's sex role concepts and attitudes. In E. E. Maccoby (Ed.), *The development of sex differences*. Stanford: Stanford University Press, 1966.

Koizumi, K. *Father And I: Memories of Lafcadio Hearn*. Boston: Houghton Mifflin, 1935.

Koutrelakos, J. Authoritarian person's perception of his relationship with his father. *Perceptual and Motor Skills*, 1968, *26*, 967-973.

Lambert, W. E., and Klineberg, O. *Children's Views of Foreign Peoples*. New York: Appleton-Century Crofts, 1967.

Landy, F., Rosenberg, B. G., and Sutton-Smith, B. The effects of limited father absence on cognitive development. *Child Development*, 1969, *40*, 941-944.

Lansky, L. M. The family structure also affects the model: Sex-role identification in parents of preschool children. *Merrill-Palmer Quarterly*, 1964, *10*, 39-50.

Le Masters, E. E. *Parents In Modern America*. Homewood, Illinois: Dorsey Press, 1970.

————— The passing of the dominant husband-father. *Impact of Science on Society*, 1971, *21* (1), 21-30.

Leonard, M. R. Fathers and daughters: The significance of "fathering" in the psychosexual development of the girl. *International Journal of Psychoanalysis*, 1966, *47*, 325-334.

Lerner, M. The vanishing American father. *McCalls*, 1965, *92* (MY), 95+.

Lessing, E. E., Zagorin, S. W., and Nelson, D. WISC subtest and IQ score correlates of father absence. *Journal of Genetic Psychology*, 1970, *117*, 181-195.

Levin, P. L. Putting down father. *New York Times Magazine*, 1965 (March 21), 79.

Levitt, E. E., and Edwards, J. A. A multivariate study of correlative factors of youthful cigarette smoking. *Developmental Psychology,* 1970, *2,* 5-11.

Levy, D. *Maternal over-protection.* New York: Columbia University Press, 1943.

Lidz, R. W., and Lidz, T. The family environment of the schizophrenic patient. *American Journal of Psychiatry,* 1949, *106,* 332-345.

Lidz, T., and Fleck, S. Schizophrenia, human integration, and the role of the family. In D. D. Jackson (Ed.), *The Etiology of Schizophrenia.* New York: Basic Books, 1960, pp. 323-45.

_____ Fleck, S., and Cornelison, A. *Schizophrenia and The Family.* New York: International Universities Press, 1966.

_____ Parker, B., and Cornelison, A. The role of the father in the family environment of the schizophrenic patient. *American Journal of Psychiatry,* 1956, *113,* 126-132.

Liebenberg, B. Expectant fathers. *American Journal of Orthopsychiatry,* 1967, *37,* 358-359.

Lifur, L. *The possibility of licensing adults to have children.* Paper presented at the meeting of the American Psychological Association, Montreal, August, 1973.

Littig, L. W., and Yeracaris, C. A. Achievement motivation and intergenerational occupational mobility. *Journal of Personality and Social Psychology,* 1965, *1,* 386-389.

Louisell, D. W., and Carroll, C. The father as non-parent. *The Catholic World,* 1969, *210,* 108-110.

Lynn, D. B. Sex-role and parental identification. *Child Development,* 1962, *33,* 555-564.

_____ Curvilinear relation between cognitive functioning and distance of child from parent of the same sex. *Psychological Review,* 1969, *76,* 236-240.

———— and Sawrey, W. L. The effects of father-absence on Norwegian boys and girls. *Journal of Abnormal and Social Psychology,* 1959, *59,* 258-262.

Maccoby, E. E. *The Development Of Sex Differences.* Stanford: Stanford University Press, 1966.

MacDonald, A. P., Jr. Internal-external locus of control: Parental Antecedents. *Journal of Consulting and Clinical Psychology,* 1971, *37,* 141-147.

Maisch, H. *Incest.* New York: Stein and Day, 1972.

Malinowski, B. *The fathers in primitive psychology.* New York: Norton, 1927.

Margetts, S. Why do executives' children run away? *Dun's Review,* 1968, *91* (JA), 40-42.

Martindale, C.ʹ Father's absence, psychopathology, and poetic eminence. *Psychological Reports,* 1972, *31,* 843-847.

Maxwell, A. E. Discrepancies between the pattern of abilities of normal and neurotic children. *Journal of Mental Science,* 1961, *107,* 300-307.

McCarry, C. *Citizen Nader.* New York: Saturday Review Press, 1972.

McClelland, D. C., Atkinson, J. W., Clark, R. A., and Lowell, E. L. *The Achievement Motive.* New York: Appleton-Century-Crofts, 1953.

———— and Watt, N. F. Sex-role alienation in schizophrenia. *Journal of Abnormal Psychology,* 1968, *73,* 226-239.

McCord, W., and McCord, J. M. *Origins of Crime: A New Evaluation of the Cambridge - Somerville Youth Study.* Montclair, New Jersey: Patterson Smith, 1969.

———— McCord, W., and Thurber, E. Some effects of paternal absence on male children. *Journal of Abnormal and Social Psychology,* 1962, *64,* 361-369.

McIntire, R. W. Parenthood training or mandatory birth control: Take your choice. *Psychology Today,* 1973, 7, 34+.

McKeown, J. E., and Chyatte, C. The behavior of fathers as reported by normals, neurotics, and schizophrenics. *American Catholic Sociological Review,* 1954, *15,* 332-340.

Mednick, S. A., Schulsinger, F., Higgins, J., and Bell, B. *Genetics, Environment, and Psychopathology.* Amsterdam: North-Holland Publishing Company, 1974.

Meet Ralph Nader, *Newsweek,* January 22, 1968.

Metraux, R. Parents and children: an analysis of contemporary German child-care and youth-guidance literature. In M. Mead and M. Wolfenstein (Eds.), *Childhood in Contemporary Cultures.* Chicago: University of Chicago Press, 1955.

Mischel, W., and Liebert, R. M. The role of power in the adoption of self-reward patterns. *Child Development,* 1967, *38,* 673-683.

Mitchell, G., Redican, W. K., and Gomber, J. Males can raise babies. *Psychology Today,* 1974, 11 (April), 63-68.

Mohr, G. J., Richmond, J. B., Garner, A. M., and Eddy, E. J. A program for the study of children with psychosomatic disorders. In G. Caplan (Ed.), *Emotional Problems of Early Childhood.* New York: Basic Books, 1955, pp. 251-268.

Monahan, T. P. Family status and the delinquent child. *Social Forces,* 1957, *35,* 250-258.

Money, J. Psychosexual differentiation. In J. Money (Ed.), *Sex Research: New Developments.* New York: Holt, Rinehart, and Winston, 1965.

Morris, P. Fathers in prison. *British Journal of Criminology,* 1967, 7, 424-430.

Moulton, R. W., Liberty, P. G., Burnstein, E., and Altucher, N. Patterning of parental affection and disciplinary dominance as a determinant of guilt and sex typing. *Journal of Personality and Social Psychology*, 1966, *4*, 356-363.

Munroe, R. L., and Munroe, R. H. Male pregnancy symptoms and cross-sex identity in three societies. *Journal of Social Psychology*, 1971, *84*, 11-25.

Mussen, P. Some antecedents and consequences of masculine sex-typing in adolescent boys. *Psychological Monographs*, 1961, *75*, No. 2.

——— and Distler, L. Child-rearing antecedents of masculine identification in kindergarten boys. *Child Development*, 1960, *31*, 89-100.

——— and Rutherford, E. Parent-child relations and parental personality in relation to young children's sex-role preferences. *Child Development*, 1963, *34*, 589-607.

Nakamura, C. Y., and Rogers, M. M. Parents' expectations of autonomous behavior and children's autonomy. *Developmental Psychology*, 1969, *1*, 613-617.

Nash, J. Fathers and sons: A neglected aspect of child-care. *Child Care*, 1952, *6*, 19-22.

——— It's time fathers got back in the family. *MacLean's* (May 12, 1956), 28-29.

——— The father in contemporary culture and current psychological literature. *Child Development*, 1965, *36*, 261-297.

O'Connor, P. J. Aetiological factors in homosexuality as seen in R.A.F. psychiatric practice. *British Journal of Psychiatry*, 1964, *110*, 381-391.

O'Gara, J. O. Oh dad, poor dad. *Commonweal*, 1962, 77, - 64.

Pauker, J. D. Fathers of children conceived out of

wedlock: Prepregnancy, high school, psychological test results. *Developmental Psychology,* 1971, *4,* 215-218.

Payne, D. E., and Mussen, P. H. Parent-child relations and father identification among adolescent boys. *Journal of Abnormal and Social Psychology,* 1956, *52,* 358-362.

Pedersen, F. A. Relationship between father absence and emotional disturbance in male military dependents. *Merrill-Palmer Quarterly,* 1966, *12,* 321-333.

——————— and Robson, K. S. Father participation in infancy. *American Journal of Orthopsychiatry,* 1969, *39,* 466-472.

Peterson, D. R., Becker, W. C., Hellmer, L. A., Shoemaker, D. J., and Quay, H. C. *Child Development,* 1959, *30,* 119-130.

Poole, K. The etiology of gender identity and the lesbian. *The Journal of Social Psychology,* 1972, *87,* 51-57.

Purcell, K., Brady, K., Chai, H., Muser, J., Molk, L., Gordon, N., and Means, J. The effect on asthma in children of experimental separation from the family. *Psychosomatic Medicine,* 1969, *31,* 144-164.

Rabkin, L. Y. The disturbed child's perception of his parents. *Journal of Individual Psychology,* 1964, *20,* - 172-178.

Rau, M. C. *Indira Priyadarshini.* New Delhi: Popular Book Services, 1966.

Roe, A. The Making Of A Scientist. New York: Dodd Mead and Co., 1953.

Rosen, B., and D'Andrade, R. The psychosocial origins of achievement motivation. *Sociometry,* 1959, *22,* 47-60.

Rosenberg, B. G., and Sutton-Smith, B. Family interaction effects on masculinity-femininity. *Journal of Personality and Social Psychology, 8,* 117-120.

Rosenberg, C. M. Determinants of psychiatric illness in young people. *British Journal of Psychiatry,* 1969, *115,* 907-915.

Rosenthal, M. J., Ni, E., Finkelstein, M., and Berkwitz, G. K. Father-child relationships and children's problems. *Archives of General Psychiatry,* 1962, *7,* 360-373.

Rothbart, M. K., and Maccoby, E. E. Parents' differential reactions to sons and daughters. *Journal of Personality and Social Psychology,* 1966, *4,* 237-243.

Rubenstein, B. O., and Levitt, M. Some observations regarding the role of fathers in child psychotherapy. *Bulletin of The Menninger Clinic,* 1957, *21,* 16-27.

Rychlak, J. F., and Legerski, A. T. A sociocultural theory of appropriate sexual role identification and level of personal adjustment. *Journal of Personality,* 1967, *35,* 31-49.

Salber, E. J., Reed, R. B., Harrison, S. V., and Grien, J. H. Smoking behavior, recreational activities and attitudes toward smoking among Newton secondary school children. *Pediatrics,* 1963, *32,* 911-918.

Santrock, J. W. Influence of onset and type of paternal absence on the first four Eriksonian Developmental Crises. *Developmental Psychology,* 1970, *3,* 273-274.

Sears, P. S. Doll-play aggression in normal young children: Influence of sex, age, sibling status, father's absence. *Psychological Monographs,* 1951, *65,* No. 6.

Sears, R. R., Maccoby, E. E., and Levin, H. *Patterns of Child Rearing.* New York: Row, Peterson, 1957.

_____ Pintler, M. H., and Sears, P. S. The effect of father separation on preschool children's doll-play aggression. *Child Development,* 1946, *17,* 219-243.

_____ Rau, L., and Alpert, R. *Identification and Child Rearing.* Stanford, Calif.: Stanford University Press, 1965.

Seeley, J. R., Sim, R. A., and Loosley, E. W. *Crestwood Heights: A Study Of The Culture Of Suburban Life.* New York: Basic Books, 1956.

Seplin, C. D. A study of the influence of the father's absence for military service. *Smith College Studies In Social Work,* 1952, *22,* 123-124 (Abstract).

Silver, L. B., Dublin, C. C., and Lourie, R. S. Does violence breed violence? Contributions from a study of the child abuse syndrome. *American Journal of Psychiatry,* 1969, *126,* 404-407.

Sopchak, A. L. Parental "identification" and "tendency toward disorders" as measured by the Minnesota Multiphasic Personality Inventory. *Journal of Abnormal and Social Psychology,* 1952, *47,* 159-165.

Spinetta, J. J., and Rigler, D. The child abusing parent: A psychological review. *Psychological Bulletin,* 1972, 77, 296-304.

Spock, B. Fathers as disciplinarians. *Redbook,* 1969, *132,* (April), 26-32.

Stafford, J. *A Mother in History.* Ferrar, Straus & Giroux, 1966.

Stephens, W. N. Judgments by social workers on boys and mothers in fatherless families. *Journal of Genetic Psychology,* 1961, *99,* 59-64.

Stolz, L. *Influences On Parent Behavior.* Stanford: Stanford University Press, 1967.

Strecker, E. A. *Their mothers' sons.* Philadelphia: J. B. Lippincott, 1951.

Strickland, B. R. Prediction of social action from a dimension of internal-external control. *Journal of Social Psychology,* 1965, *66,* 353-358.

Suedfeld, P. Paternal absence and overseas success of Peace Corps volunteers. *Journal of Consulting Psychology,* 1967, *31,* 424-425.

Suinn, R. M. The relationship between self-acceptance

and acceptance of others: A learning theory analysis. *Journal of Abnormal and Social Psychology*, 1961, *63*, 37-42.

Sutherland, H. E. G. The relationship between I.Q. and size of family in the case of fatherless children. *Journal of Genetic Psychology*, 1930, *38*, 161-170.

Sutton-Smith, B., Roberts, J. M., and Rosenberg, B. G. Sibling associations and role involvement. *Merrill-Palmer Quarterly*, 1964, *10*, 25-38.

_____ and Rosenberg, B. G. *The Sibling*. New York: Holt, Rinehart, and Winston, Inc., 1970.

_____ Rosenberg, B. G., and Landy, F. Father-absence effects in families of different sibling compositions. *Child Development*, 1968, *39*, 1213-1221.

Taboroff, L. H., and Brown, W. N. A study of the personality patterns of children and adolescents with the peptic ulcer syndrome. *American Journal of Orthopsychiatry*, 1954, *24*, 602-610.

Tallman, I. Spousal role differentiation and the socialization of severely retarded children. *Journal of Marriage and The Family*, 1965, *27*, 37-42.

Tasch, R. J. The role of the father in the family. *Journal of Experimental Education*, 1952, *20*, 319-361.

Tauris, C. Who likes women's liberation—and why: The case of the unliberated liberals. *Journal of Social Issues*, 1973, *29*, 175-198.

Thomes, M. M. Children with absent fathers. *Journal of Marriage and The Family*, 1968, *30*, 89-96.

Toby, J. The differential impact of family disorganization. *American Sociological Review*, 1957, *22*, 505-512.

Trunnell, T. L. The absent father's children's emotional disturbances. *Archives of General Psychiatry*, 1968, *19*, 180-188.

Turner, J. H. Entrepreneurial environments and the emergence of achievement motivation in adolescent males. *Sociometry,* 1970, *33,* 147-165.

Van Manen, G. C. Father roles and adolescent socialization. *Adolescence,* 1968, *3,* 139-152.

Vincent, C. E. *Unmarried Mothers.* New York: Free Press of Glencoe, 1961.

Wainwright, W. H. Fatherhood as a precipitant of mental illness. *American Journal of Psychiatry,* 1966, *123,* 40-44.

Warren, E. (Chairman). *Report of The President's Commission on the Assassination of President John F. Kennedy.* Washington, D.C.: U. S. Government Printing Office, 1964.

Weisberg, P. S., and Springer, K. J. Environmental factors in creative function. In R. L. Mooney and T. A. Razik (Eds.), *Exploration In Creativity.* New York: Harper and Row, 1967, pp. 120-134.

Werts, C. E. Paternal influence on career choice. *Journal of Counseling Psychology,* 1968, *15,* 48-52.

West, D. J. Parental relationships in male homosexuality. *International Journal of Social Psychiatry,* 1959, *5,* - 85-97.

Westwood, G. A. *A Minority Report On The Life Of The Male Homosexual In Great Britain.* London: Longmans, Green, 1960.

White, B. J. The relationship of self-concept and parental identification to women's vocational interests. *Journal of Counseling Psychology,* 1959, *6,* 202-206.

Williams, A. F. Personality and other characteristics associated with cigarette smoking among young teenagers. *Journal of Health and Social Behavior,* 1973, *14,* 374-380.

Winch, R. Some data bearing on the Oedipal hypothesis.

Journal of Abnormal and Social Psychology, 1950, *45*, 481-489.

Winterbottom, M. R. The relation of need for achievement to learning experiences in independence and mastery. In J. W. Atkinson (Ed.), *Motives in Fantasy, Action, and Society*. Princeton: Van Nostrand, 1958, pp. 453-78.

Wolman, B. B. *Children Without Childhood*. New York: Grune and Stratton, 1970.

_____ Schizophrenia in childhood. In B. B. Wolman (Ed.), *Manual of Child Psychopathology*. New York: McGraw-Hill Co., 1972.

Wright, B., and Tuska, S. The nature and origin of feeling feminine. *British Journal of Social and Clinical Psychology*, 1966, *5*, 140-149.

index

Levitt, M., 3
Liberty, P. G., 59
Lidz, R. W., 130
Lidz, T., 126, 130
Liebenberg, B., 9
Liebert, R. M., 61
Lifur, L., 155–157
Lindzey, G., 79
Littig, L. W., 105
Lorge-Thorndike intelligence
    test, 42
Louisell, D. W., 1
Lourie, R. S., 108

McAdoo, W. G., 64
McCarry, C., 116–118
McClelland, D. C. 70, 102, 128
Maccoby, E. E., 15, 92
McCord, J. M., 21
McCord, W., 21
MacDonald, A. P., 114–116
McIntire, Roger W., 155–156
McKeown, J. E., 126–127
Maisch, H., 97
Margetts, S., 5
Martindale, C., 70
Masculinity-Femininity. *See*
    Identification; Sex-role
    development
Mass media, 146–148
Maxwell, A. E., 38
Mentally retarded, 75
Metraux, R., 3
Mischel, W., 61
Mitchell, G., 10
MMPI, 26, 83
Mohr, G. J., 138
Monahan, T. P., 22
Monkeys, paternal behavior in,
    10
Moral development, 13, 27
Mother absence, 6

delinquency, 21, 71
    success in military, 25
    success in Peace Corps, 25
    suicide, 23
Moulton, R. W., 59
Munroe, R. H., 8
Munroe, R. L., 8
Mussen, P. H., 56–57, 89

Nader, Laura, 116–118
Nader, Nathra, 116–118
Nader, Ralph, 116–118
Nader, Rose, 117–118
Nader, Shaffak, 116–118
Nakamura, C. Y., 90–91
Nash, J., 1
Nehru, Jawaharlal, 97–99
Nelson, D., 38–39
Neurotics, 67–68, 69–70, 127–28,
    130, 132–133
Ni, E., 133–137

Occupation of father, 7, 12–13,
    16–17, 22, 23, 41, 45, 55,
    112, 165, 169
    son's achievement motivation,
    104
    son's occupation, 75, 112, 120
O'Connor, P. J., 64
Oedipal conflict, 37, 53–54
    for females, 79–80
O'Gara, J. O., 7–8
Ommission of father in studies,
    2
Orr, H. K., 74
Oswald, Lee Harvey, 46–50
Oswald, Marguerite, 46–50

Parental sex roles and child
    adjustment, 68, 69–70
Parker, J. D., 126
Parsons, Talcott, 81